Green Glass Beads

and Merryl's Poetry

MERRYLYNN COX

authorHOUSE®

AuthorHouse™
1663 Liberty Drive
Bloomington, IN 47403
www.authorhouse.com
Phone: 1 (800) 839-8640

Published by AuthorHouse 11/07/2019

ISBN: 978-1-7283-3166-9 (sc)
ISBN: 978-1-7283-3167-6 (e)

Print information available on the last page.

This book is printed on acid-free paper.

Dedicated to "my merry sunshine"

A wise son is the joy of his mother.
— Proverb of Solomon

Today Merryl felt like a four-time loser. Besides an alienated married son, she had a daughter in the hospital's psychiatric unit, a run-away son somewhere in New Mexico, and a young Ms. on the verge of high school, independence, and rebellion. Today she felt condemned to a life of guilt for her failings as a mother, sentenced to a job she didn't want, now threatened with layoff, and bound in marriage to an unstable man who wasn't working . . . again. But all in the world Merryl wanted today was a string of green glass beads—a very specific string of green glass beads. The memory of them seemed to her the only embodiment of warmth and love.

Merryl was forty-six and tired of teenagers, tired of working, tired of marriage. The downtown graffiti she had seen from the bus had become her unconscious philosophy: Life's a bitch and then you die. She knew that wasn't all there was to it, but that was exactly how she felt much of the time. Those scrawled words had ended, incongruously, with a spark of indomitable hope—Have a nice day. Remembering, she resolved to try.

As she struggled to make the ironing board stand up one more time, it seemed this day was going to be more than she could bear. "Come on," she cajoled grimly. "If you will stand up one more time, I will never fold you up again!" The poor old ironing board had found itself in the way of several outbursts of frustration from the man of the house. It was tired, like Merryl, but she was determined to press her new pink blouse.

As she shook and pulled and rattled the ironing board into a standing position, she relived standing at Penney's mail order counter the night before with held breath as the clerk ran the charge ticket through. She knew that she was right at her limit again and wasn't sure if she could squeeze through one more seven-dollar item. *I really shouldn't get it anyway*, she thought feeling shamefully self-indulgent. *I have two daughters who need clothes, but it is on sale, and it is such a pretty pink.*

"Finally! Now please stand there a minute," she pleaded with the ironing board as she began to press the packaging creases out of her new blouse. *It's just right for perking up that old gray suit. I'm glad I got it . . . even if I can't afford it.*

In the bathroom, the comforting warmth of the sudsy water on her face brought forth a spontaneous prayer of gratitude. *Ah! Thank you for warm water! And Friday! And pay day! And new pink blouses! Your grace is sufficient for me. Somehow, I'll get through this day, too.*

Merryl was running late. As she had reached to push

in the alarm button, her exhausted husband roused from his brief sleep, turned over, and proceeded to recount to her again how unhappy he was. *I'll just have to say my prayers on the bus*, Merryl reconciled. Larry's early morning words rested heavily on her. *It's not just that horrible temporary janitorial job that's making him miserable. He's always miserable.* The thought *How can I carry all this?* seemed to weigh her movements into slow motion as she dressed.

Ten minutes to bus time. I've got to fly like the wind! Oh, they never make these bows to tie right! But it's a cheapie. Uh oh, it's going to rain. I don't have time to go back for my raincoat. Maybe I can make it to the bus before it does.

As she walked briskly, the light sprinkle felt good. It had been hotter the past week than it had been in years — well over 100 degrees for four days in a row. Even at 7 a.m., it had been nearly 90 all week for these sprints to the bus stop. The refreshing sprinkle fell on Merryl's wilting spirit; it sprang up with instant rehydration. *Hallowed by Thy name, Father. Thy kingdom come, Thy will be done, Father, in my home, in my marriage, in my family, as it is in Heaven. Oh, I want those green glass beads.* They were so desperately tangible before her out of the twenty-year past, she could almost put them around her neck. *Oh, I want those beads back! I want that little boy back! I want to live that day over again and do it right this time!* The concern about the impending layoff was eclipsed by this more pressing matter.

Running through the ever-lengthening list of needs of her disjoined family fully occupied Merryl on her trip downtown until the bus deposited her in the shadow of the fifty-story office building where she would spend her day. *I forgot, this shoe squeaks! Darn!* Merryl was in metamorphosis, undergoing the transformation from one realm of her life to the other while pulling off her walking shoes and slipping into her high heels. The ride up the elevator into the sky of Tulsa every morning was like a trip through the looking glass, a shedding of skin, problems, wishes, feelings. She stepped out of the elevator into the practical corporate world of flawlessly groomed, perfectly performing secretaries. There was no room here for personal problems. She merged with the stream of men and women, all looking much alike in their neutral business suits, filing to their places.

Still, personal problems persisted, even in this efficient environment. *The drizzle ruined my hair, and Krista took my hairspray out of my tote bag again! Oh well, what does it matter what I look like anyway.* A wave of self-pity inundated her. *God, I don't want to be here. Why do I have to go on every day? I wish there were no more days! I'd like to stop the world and get off!*

As she turned in her swivel chair to take the vinyl cover off her typewriter, she fervently wished she'd never learned to type. She sat with her hands in her lap staring at the keyboard. She had arrived before her boss, and it was quiet in the office — a nice place really. No one, not her husband, or her mother, or friends, could understand why she didn't love this job. Clean office with good lighting, live plants, carpet, and nice people, most of them. Her heart just wasn't in it. This wasn't her element. That very first day she stepped off the elevator onto the twenty-ninth floor of the glass and steel tower, she felt she was stepping out onto another planet. This was an alien world to her. She never lost the feeling of being out of her natural habitat, a stranger in a strange land.

I want to be back there. I want to go back and live that day over. Why can't I get past it? Why has it become so important to me again? Her mind began winging its way back over the years and miles to another summer day. She was much younger but already harried by life's turbulence. She was there in the little house that was so much like all the other little rent houses they had lived in over the years. The baby cried in her crib, and dirty dishes filled the sink. Her heart felt the same enormous, all-pervading void — too cold and gray to be called pain. A void, that's all it was . . . a huge, vacant void.

That long-ago conversation with her next-door neighbor replayed in her mind. They were face to face again over the backyard fence, her clothespins in hand. *What was it she said?* "Why, if my husband was ever unfaithful, I'd kill him!" *She didn't know what it was like and probably never would. She was a tacky, awful woman but so damn sure of herself. A fat, bleached slob! I never told her. I would never let her know I couldn't hold a man's devotion as well as she could. How did she do it anyway? I tried to be so good to my husband. I really wanted so little — just to take care of my home and kids. How could she charge that little guy fifty cents for those junky beads? Fifteen cents would have been plenty. Brent worked all morning, I found out, to gather together fifty cents. That was a lot of money, even to me, in those days.*

Those days! What was so different about those days? I don't have fifty cents to my name today. Mr. Doom and Gloom is still at it, complaining and miserable. Larry was out of work then, too, wasn't he? I don't know if they called it fired or laid off. Just like this time, he says he quit, but that's not what some of the others say.

The phone ringing at her elbow startled Merryl out of her reverie. Habitually, the efficient secretary persona took over. "Good morning, National Sales. This is Merryl."

"Did you know we're out of milk?" said the tense, angry voice on the other end of the line."

"No, I'm sorry, I didn't. No one told me."

"Why don't you check those things? My stomach's burnin' and there's no damn milk!"

"I'm sorry, Larry. I didn't notice."

"Dammit! I've gotta go do those damn hardwax floors again all night, and you don't even care."

"Please, just go get some milk."

"You're such a god-damn bitch! Hell, I don't think I've ever been this unhappy. I just can't go on. I just don't have it in me anymore."

"You've said that for years. You can do what you have to, like I have to. I get my check today. I'll go get milk tonight. Oh, but you'll have the car."

"Forget it, just forget it!"

Slam! and silence from the phone on the other end. Merryl sat feebly holding the receiver. *I wonder if crying would help*, she sighed. *I wish I could just cry it all away.*

She quietly slipped the receiver into its cradle. *Why go on? Why? I wish I could have a nice little nervous breakdown — nothing serious, six months or so in a padded cell. But what else can I do but keep on keepin' on.*

Merryl braced both hands wearily against the desk and hoisted herself to a standing position, slowly and painfully, like one stiff with the years. *Eight-thirty already. I've got to get the mail. Where's that smile? I'll need to paste one on to get through the morning. I'll go to the Body Shop at lunch for aerobics, then I'll feel better.* The warming thought of moving her ancient feeling muscles to the music for thirty minutes at lunch time soothed and relaxed her mood for a moment. Then even that fleeting hope vanished as she remembered, *Drat, I can't go today. I have to take my check to the bank and then get that birthday present for Tami's party. I promised Krista. Rats! Forget that smile. I'm going without one today!*

Time passed, bit by bit, as time will, until a morning's gone, and then a day, and then twenty years. Crossing the plaza, Merryl clutched her sack lunch but had no real appetite for the tuna salad sandwich and orange sections she brought from home. She had been lucky in her quest for Tami's birthday present. In fact, she was so pleased with her $1.99 bargain — three shades of eye shadow in a cute little mirrored compact — she bought three. Her budding glamour girls would like them, too. She'd stash her find to help ease the next Christmas financial crisis that would so soon be upon her.

Buying the birthday present hadn't taken as long as she thought it would, and she had a few minutes to relax and eat her lunch. She found an empty bench. The plaza was almost deserted today; it was sizzling, even in the shade — too hot for those who didn't have to be out. There was the street preacher, though. He was always there on the corner at noon in dress shirt, suit, and tie. How did he stand it?

Merryl had been carrying her suit jacket and now draped it carefully over the back of the green wooden bench. The pink bow of her blouse fluttered as she sat down. *I really love this pink,* she thought as she smiled inside. She allowed the rosy color to fill up her senses and circulate through her fibers like wine. She closed her eyes and tilted her head back, shaking the damp hair off of the back of her neck. It felt good to sit there, in the open. The sparse shade gave little relief from the sun, but she really didn't mind. She preferred it to the office, all shut up and artificial. *Climate control. I prefer the "seasons of the day."* That phrase always took her back to the time she coined it for herself in that hot little duplex, the second year of their marriage. The evenings were always so welcome when you had to endure the heat of the day without climate control.

As she inhaled her moment of solitude, the quiet feeling of the dappled sun and shade on her upturned face brought a vivid image to her mind's eye. It was as fresh as ever — Brent, almost a year old, standing at the screen door, fat little bare feet and legs, round tummy hanging over his diaper, one hand holding the doorframe to steady himself; he was barely walking. The low evening sun through the trees in the front yard was lighting up the strands of his blond curls like glowing filaments, giving a halo aura to the crown of his baby head. A cherub if ever there was one. Merryl reveled in the image for a long, wonderful moment.

Without warning, a pang caught her in the throat, an ache of uncontrollable intensity. *I would never have done anything to hurt him. How could I have been so cruel?* She snatched up her jacket and lunch sack before the tears came and bolted for the intersection. While she was waiting for the walk light, the booming voice of the pacing preacher reached her ears from the corner. "Love never fails," he was shouting, "God is love, and God can't fail, so love can't never fail, not never!" Merryl turned to see his shining black, bald head glistening with sweat in the sun. *He really believes that*, Merryl marveled, drawn into the passion of his expression.

The furrows of his forehead, the intense bushy, graying eyebrows, the broad pumping nostrils, the full lips were all committed to the vital importance of conveying his message to the disinterested noontime pedestrians. His open Bible flapped its white pages in the air as if it would fly as he waved it over his head toward the blaring blue summer sky. Merryl stared, feeling the tightness in her throat subsiding, *I think I believe it, too,* she mulled, *but why is love failing? I'm failing in everything about love.*

Suddenly she was aware that she was standing still on the curb by herself as several passersby rushed around her. The traffic light had changed, and she hadn't noticed. She collected herself and scurried across the street as the Walk changed to Wait again. She shivered with a chill as she entered the cool office building. Her skin was damp from the walk in the hot, humid air, so she stopped by the dress shop to slip her jacket on before heading for the elevator.

There it was. That suit on the mannequin in Casual Corner's window was what caught her eye the day before. That gorgeous Kelly green caused the wheels of her brain to scheme and calculate to see if there could be any possibility of putting it in layaway and getting it out by fall. But it was those beads around the neck of the window dummy that broke into her scheming. Like a specter from the past, they reminded her of what she had done. She tried not to think about that for years — since they moved from that little house. It tormented her so that she had to stop thinking about it. But it hadn't gone away, none of it . . . none of the pain, none of the regret.

Those beads are so much like mine. Mine? Oh, I <u>wish</u> they were mine. They <u>could</u> have been mine. They were supposed to *be mine. I think I threw them away. Oh God, did I? I couldn't stand to look at them after what I did. I don't have any idea what happened to them. Maybe Brent threw them away. I wouldn't wonder if he did! What I said was like a slap in the face to him! To that six-year-old boy, those cheap green beads were really beautiful. I didn't know till he told me years later how he scrounged and planned to scrape together fifty cents to buy those "beautiful" beads for me. He told me how he looked under the couch cushions and along the curb for pennies. He returned some pop bottles and ran an errand for Grandpa, and I don't remember what all he said. It was a project of love for me! That hussy, if she'd had any decency at all, she would have asked him to pay only fifteen cents, instead of fifty cents. Why was that all I saw at that moment — me, who always treasured every dandelion gift brought in childish delight? How could I have dashed him down from his accomplishment the way I did?*

Merryl stood transfixed across from the inner window of the dress shop. The lunch rush was past, and the few stragglers in the building lobby paid no attention to her. She wasn't there at all; it was no longer 1987. She stood in the tiny disorderly living room of the little crackerbox house. The sofabed where Brent slept was still pulled out, unmade, though it was after noon. The tension hung in the room from the recent argument.

She caught him. Larry lied to her, and she found out. He hadn't been with Bill like he said. Bill called for him at the house. Then she knew. He was with that girl, the one he met in therapy at the psych center, where they diagnosed him as bipolar after that first suicide attempt. She remembered the raw hurt in her heart the way it felt that day . . . that summer day when Brent brought her the green glass beads.

She meant to go over to the garage sale next door as a neighborly courtesy, but she was too busy with the new baby. Merryl stood in the kitchen doorway again between the pile of dirty dishes in the kitchen sink and the full laundry baskets and the unmade sofa bed in the living room. She felt the fierce Oklahoma August heat roaring in through both the open front and back doors. All the windows were open, too. She had moved the large roll-around fan into the tiny back bedroom to help the baby sleep, so there wasn't enough air moving through the kitchen and living room to stir the light curtain panels. The neighbors probably heard their angry words. Larry had stalked off into their bedroom and left her standing there, taut, frustrated, feeling that her entire world was a mess.

If I ever needed love in my life, that was the moment, Merryl remembered. *How could I have been so unkind, unfeeling, unappreciative to blurt out such a thing!* As if to torture herself in punishment, Merryl began reliving, again, every detail of the pain she had felt so many times in replaying the memory, twisting the knife deeper and deeper. She couldn't hurt enough to pay for her ruthlessness.

There is that little boy again, six years old, coming up the front steps, the glaring sun behind him, lighting his sunshine hair as he reaches up to open the screen door. How many times she had delighted in those sunshine curls and that sunshine smile. "My merry sunshine" she called him. He moves toward her a little shyly, self-consciously, grinning, showing his missing front teeth. One tennis shoe is untied, and the sock is disappearing into his shoe. He has a dirty child-sized hand print on the front of his striped polo shirt and a Super-Hero Band-aid on his knee below his shorts.

From behind his back he proudly produces the string of green beads — a set of bright green, graduated, opaque, glass beads. "I bought these for you at the garage sale," he says in a soft voice.

God, can't I go back and do this again? Can't I say something else this time, please? Can't I ever do this over again? Whatever made me ask, "How much?" What did it matter how much? Even to a family with two small children and no income, how could it have possibly mattered how much?

"Fifty cents," was his honest reply, not knowing either how it could matter.

God, I can't say it again. Please let me kneel down and put my arms around him this time. I want to give that beautiful little boy such a hug. I can feel how it should have been. I would take him into my arms smiling into his smile, drawing him close to me, hugging him tight, kissing his happy little cheeks. "Oh, thank you honey," I'd say. "They're wonderful! How did you ever get fifty cents to buy me such a beautiful present? You're a precious boy. You make me so happy. I love you so much." Then I'd hug him again and feel his hair against my face and turn to kiss it, and then squeeze him once more. Then I'd gratefully receive his gift as I had received his love and put the cheap, gaudy things around my neck and wear them all day, so he could see how important they were to me. Can't I do it that way this time please, God?

"She charged you fifty cents for those? They're not worth ten!"

No, I didn't say it. I couldn't have. How could I have said that? I was so mad at her, that short, fat, immature, bleached blonde — financially secure, apparently stable marriage. I was so envious. Why not me? I had the small baby, the son who needed a father. I was hurting so. I needed what she had. She didn't need it or deserve it.

But what happened to those green glass beads? I don't remember. Did he place them in my hands anyway, or did he take them with him when he turned around and walked back out the front screen door? All I remember is the disappearance of his grin . . . the way the smile vanished from his eyes. I felt his pain. From his drooping head and shoulders, I felt it. After twenty years I still feel it. Did he go cry? Was he very angry? Did he have any idea of the turmoil that was going on inside me that day? How long did he hate me? I knew I had done a terrible wrong, but I was too dead inside to care about his hurt at that moment, and that's what's killing me. Of all the sins of my life, that's the only one I still remember. I cringe to think that it might be still as fresh for him as it is for me. I wonder if maturity and adult understanding have eased it any. He was always so forgiving. That day that I yelled at him when he was so little, three maybe, I apologized to him when I tucked him into bed that night. In his bright, sweet, baby voice he said, "That's all right, Mommy." But this was too big! Too cruel. There's no getting over it or getting past it, ever.

Merryl's own sob wrenched her back into the present. *I'm late! I never even ate my lunch. I've got to get back upstairs. My gosh, how long have I been standing here? I'm getting crazy. Maybe I am having that breakdown*, Merryl thought in her frenzy as she dashed for the elevator.

In the afternoon mail was the news they'd all been waiting for. The sale was going through, and the company would be moving. They'd all be out of jobs soon. To Merryl, it felt more like relief than tragedy, but they had to eat. Maybe it was Larry's turn to earn the full-time income again for a while. Who was she kidding? She'd have to find another job, but she couldn't think about that today. Nothing but those beads filled her head today.

At five o'clock, as Merryl covered her typewriter, the phone rang. *If I answer that, I'm liable to miss the bus*, she debated, *but if I don't, I could be in trouble.* Reluctantly, she grabbed the receiver.

"Mom, did you get the birthday present?" chirped Krista, her youngest.

"Yes, honey, but I've got to hurry, or I'll miss the bus. I'll tell you about it when I get home. I think you'll like it."

"Guess what, Scotty called."

"Scotty called? Where from?"

"I don't know — long distance. He said the Santa Fe police are going to put him on a bus for Albuquerque, and he'll be home tomorrow. Something he heard about the bus company bringing runaways home free if they'd go to the police station. Anyway, he'll be home tomorrow."

"Are you sure? How come? Who told him? Are you sure?"

"That's all he said. Said he forgot about the time difference. It's earlier there or something. Anyway, he said to tell you."

"I can hardly believe it. Gosh, I've got to go if I'm going to catch the bus. I'll be home in a little bit."

Waiting for the 5:20 bus, the weary downtown office workers clustered in the precious shade. The west sun bore down on the concrete sidewalk until heat rose in waves from the sparkling quartz crystals. Merryl stopped on the shady side of the hotel corner. She had a good view of the bus's approach, and leaning against the cool alabaster wall was mildly refreshing. In the two-block walk from the air-conditioned office, she had already begun to feel the rivulets of moisture trickling down between her shoulder blades and breasts. What had happened to that promise of rain this morning? The heat wave was unabated. The barely moving air felt as if it were being emitted from Vulcan's furnace.

A chipper voice seemed to be directed to her. "Hot enough for you?" Merryl squinted in the direction of the sun, curious to see who could sound so cheery at this time of day in this heat.

"Hi, Mr. Shrum. I surely wouldn't want it any hotter."

"That few drops of rain we got this morning didn't help much did it? Gave us just enough moisture to steam us in our own juice!"

"Oh, that's just what my grandmother used to say." Merryl managed a sociable laugh.

"I s'pose we shouldn't complain. In six months when it's zero and snowing, we'll wish we'd bottled some of this!" Those within hearing chuckled at the thought as the bus rounded the corner. All the Route Sixteen riders began to shuffle out of their shade shelter and across the glaring sidewalk to the curb. Inside the bus it was cool, at least, and by walking an extra block to the beginning of the bus line at the hotel, she had managed to get a seat. Merryl arranged her purse and bag on her lap and settled back to unwind from the day.

Scott's coming home! Thank God! Wonder how he's managed on his own for a month. Must have been rough. Bless that bus company! Running away from Dad, just like Brent did, but Brent was lots older than sixteen. I hope he can work things out better this time. He's really a sweet boy, but he looks ridiculous as a skinhead. No one would think he's sweet to look at him. I couldn't believe he even shaved off his eyebrows. The day he came by the office to tell me he was leaving, he looked like something from outer space. God, I'll be glad when he outgrows this. And I thought Brent's teenage years were rough!

Mixed up memories of her two sons' adolescent struggles swirled in her mind. Those boys were so different. The older had straight straw-colored hair, blue-gray eyes, was outgoing, athletic, a fighter; the younger had dark eyes, dark curly hair, *in the days when he had hair,* Merryl reminisced. Scott was soft spoken, gentle, non-combative, but rebellious just the same. They were both full of anger toward a father who had never grown up himself. One thing they had in common in her memory was the Juvenile Detention Center courtroom where angry boys end up, the lawyers, the fines, the weekly meetings with probation officers.

When Brent was seventeen, it had looked as though he were headed for the penitentiary. In that fight after the football game, he slashed a boy's leather jacket with a corkscrew he used to open a wine bottle. She couldn't blame the boy's parents for being upset, but the authorities were going to try Brent as an adult because he had been in trouble for the same kind of thing before when he broke his hand on a boy who came at him with a tire tool. He didn't know either boy; he was just always ready for a fight.

Merryl prayed desperately for her son. She knew he was guilty of the assault charge and that conviction and prison were certain without a miracle. Luckily, Merryl had always believed in miracles. She watched with awe as God parted the Red Sea for her son and led him across on dry land. The court docket got so full that the minor cases were dismissed, just like that. There was no trial, no sentencing. It was a miracle, that's all, a sovereign intervention of a powerful, loving God. *You've got to believe in miracles to raise teenage boys*, Merryl declared to herself as the rhythm of the bus ride rested her into reverie.

Merryl remembered Brent's subsequent mandatory counseling sessions. She tried to get him to blame his violent nature on his dad, but he never would. "I make my own choices," he insisted bravely. *How did he know that so young?* Merryl pondered, *which was it, Hercules or Apollo?—one of those guys from high school Latin mythology was pardoned by the gods because he refused his option to put the blame for his sins on circumstances or other people. Brent accepted the full responsibility for his actions, too, just like that god had done. Brent had the character of a god! Actually, some of them were pretty raunchy characters, as I recall.* Merryl had to chuckle at the thought of Brent being like a god in both ways. For all the trouble, Brent really was special. He was so smart in high school, he had to skip classes to keep from being branded with a reputation for setting the curve. *What an un-cool thing that would have been!* Merryl grimaced visibly from a reluctant degree of insight into the masculine teenage mystique.

Brent was something else. I realize that now. When he was twelve or thirteen and took on his first paper route, he'd be in bed by nine o'clock on Saturday night no matter what was going on, in order to be up by 4:30 on Sunday morning. Even in the winter, he'd get up by himself, bundle up, go out in the dark on his bike, sometimes with snow on the ground. He'd fold his papers on the curb in the park, then throw from that little bike about a hundred big morning papers in the freezing temperatures. *How did he do it? Even though I helped him in the car on a couple of the very coldest days, I really didn't realize how hard working and tough he was!*

Though always a relentless tease, Brent was goodhearted and reliable, but, mainly, Brent was just really tough. He had great determination. When he started lifting weights in high school, he figured out his own body-building plan, and nothing could keep him from his training schedule. It took priority over everything in life. He wouldn't drink a Coke or eat a biscuit or anything that wasn't good for his beautiful bod. His thighs became so muscular, he could hardly get his jeans on. *I thought we were going to have to have his pants special made. At least his devotion to body building kept him away from marijuana. I wish I could say the same for Scott.*

Brent was always an industrious little guy. As he grew, he built tree houses and dug foxholes and collected fossils. He was the boy, his first-grade teacher told Merryl, who always "had a better idea" about everything. Merryl remembered how in grade school, he used to make wonderful "inventions" by nailing bottle caps, bits of Crayola-colored wood, propellers, plastic rings, rubber bands, bicycle reflectors, and whatever to a board or a box to make fantastic-looking control panels or machines that could theoretically manage anything from time travel to clone production. He was always cooking up something — a backyard super highway, a mammoth family fireworks display, a motorized Erector Set amusement park, and wowed them with his fourth-grade paper mache' Indian totem pole.

Brent went through a memorable web-building stage at about ten. He'd loop a thousand-foot ball of kite string back and forth across the entire living room/dining area from table leg to couch leg, from couch leg to chair leg, from chair leg to stereo console leg, back and forth, this way and that, until he ran out of string, and the area looked like giant string art. It was wonderful to behold—a room-sized web. Merryl always objected because, of course, it made the front door and the room in general inaccessible. Nevertheless, she always wished she had taken a photograph of one of his giant webs before she made him unwind it. The picture in her mind remained as vivid as any snapshot could be; she hoped it was like that for him.

Merryl was so busy in those days, she missed most of Brent's school's PTA meetings. But what hurt was missing those snapshots she could never go back and take. Merryl remembered the football, wrestling team, and weightlifting pictures she wanted to take of him in high school, but she was always so concerned about embarrassing him, she took them from great distances and never got good ones. He'd love to have them now to show his own little son.

When Brent was ten, Scotty was a baby, and Bessie was about three. Merryl hadn't even realized Brent couldn't see well until his teacher pointed it out to her. When he got his first glasses, she remembered his amazement that trees had individual leaves on them. He saw them only as blurs of green up to that time. What kind of a mother was she anyway? Had she been totally negligent? Was all her hard work spent on the wrong things?

I did take time out of that busy Saturday, when he was four, to help him build that snowman. As always, I had the week's errands and grocery shopping to do, plus the housecleaning and the laundry, but, most important, we had to go out in that fresh snow that afternoon to make a snowman. It was a dandy one, too. We put Brent's little straw hat on it and a muffler. It had a carrot nose, raisin eyes and smile, and little dry branches for arms. We named him and talked to him. I took their picture together, and we had great fun for an hour or so. When I had to get back to my work, Brent didn't want to come in. He begged me to stay and play a little longer. There was no one else—no brother or sister, no playmate in the neighborhood. Duty tore me away too soon. Back in the duplex, I had no sooner taken off my coat and gloves than I looked out the front window to see Brent kicking our wonderful snowman to pieces. Daddy didn't even get to see it. How sad that made me feel to leave him so frustrated. It was my loss as well. Of course, Merryl realized in an effort at self-soothing, Brent had her more or less exclusive evening and weekend attention for almost seven years before the second child was born. She probably read him more stories and nursery rhymes than she read to the other three put together.

But she had to resume her job when Brent was only two weeks old, and it took her six months to get over the toxemia complications of pregnancy. That wholesale poisoning of her system robbed all her strength. She had no trouble losing the pregnancy weight; she became a shadow of herself, a semi-invalid with a tiny baby and a full-time secretarial job to go back to. Larry was a college student, and her job was their only income to live on. He worked as a waiter in a steak house at night, but that money was not even keeping up with the tuition which kept increasing every semester. *How did we manage to make it?* Merryl wondered as she looked back. *We were all tougher than we knew.*

Larry's mom took care of Brent for the first few years. Merryl was incredibly jealous of her. She wanted to do it herself more that she wanted to live. Those first few months, she never saw her Baby Brent awake. She had to admit the arrangement was good for Brent, though. He might have been deprived of her mothering, but at least he had something. He was definitely loved! It was just that she always felt a little replaced. But she couldn't deny her son the relationship with Grams and Grandpa that seemed to become deeper to him than his relationship with his own parents. As soon as Brent was able to toddle, he followed in Grandpa's tracks, like a puppy, everywhere he went, up and down the backyard garden rows and behind the lawnmower around and around the big fenced yard. They adored each other.

But Merryl didn't always like the way Grams took care of little Brent. When he started solid food, she discovered that Grams was mixing his strained carrots, peas, chicken, applesauce, and whatever all together in one dish for her convenience and feeding him the muddy-colored mess as one concoction. *When I suggested that it would be good if he could taste each different food separately, she let me know that I could just take him someplace else, if I didn't like it! I could have wrung her neck! I didn't have any say so in how my little boy was cared for! Keeping Larry in college classes was ALL we could manage on our measly incomes.*

But Grams was in her element when Brent had a mild case of pneumonia at about two. She was never happier than when she had someone to "doctor!" She made a very big deal of it. But he was really a robust little kid. The only other times he was sick was when his tonsils acted up a few times during those first few winters. Merryl remembered how his fever shot up so alarmingly to 104, and he was so little and listless, looking at her with such feverish, glassy, blue-gray eyes. But after he was four, and those nasty old tonsils were taken out, he was never really sick again. Not until that appendix flared up.

Somewhere along in there, Grams got tired of having to get up five days a week to babysit. She often called us at 7:30 a.m. just as Larry was leaving to take me to work and drop Brent off at her house and head to his classes, saying she "wasn't able." Then one of us would have to call in to work or skip classes to stay home with him. So, on one of those days, pre-school Brent and I walked from our duplex on 12th and Atlanta over to Villa Theresa day nursery on 15th Street to sign him up. He was a bit alarmed at first at the sisters in their long black and white garb, but they were very good to him, and he really enjoyed being around other kids his age. It was hard to cover that extra expense. Merryl couldn't remember quite how they had managed it. *I suppose I must have come up with some kind of a little raise on that secretarial job over the years! Anyway, it was great timing for Brent as preparation for kindergarten. God always has been a really good planner!* Merryl reflected with a sense of secure satisfaction.

It was in that little duplex that they spent all those struggling years getting Larry through college. He almost gave up just before his graduation. *One spring afternoon while I was at work, Larry dumped all his expensive text books and class notes in the trash barrel in that little back yard and lit a match to it. I never was sure what final frustration drove him to do that, but that was surely the pinnacle of frustration for me! After setting aside my own education for his and working all those years to that end while missing out on all those precious baby days with Brent for the sake of that degree, I could not go on if it was all for nothing. I told him that if he wanted me in his life, he would borrow books and notes and take those last finals and graduate, or I was through with him and all the struggle!*

And wonder of wonders, he did it. He somehow screwed up his will and cleared the final hurdle and graduated! Phew! We had sacrificed so much and put such hope into what that art degree would mean to our family's future! There was no hope left for us if he let all that effort, all those dreams, go down the drain.

Through all that, I didn't notice at the time how good Brent was. When he was just a little guy, he'd always brush his teeth without being told. It really paid off, too. He never had a cavity. I practically had to club Scott and drag him by his hair to get him to brush his teeth. I must have dropped the ball somewhere by the third one. It didn't seem like I was doing anything different, but Scott always seemed so much younger than Brent was at the same age; he must have been babied more.

There was ten years' difference between the boys. By the time Scott was a Cub Scout, Brent was more like a dad to Scott than his dad was. Brent took him out in the country and helped him launch his Estes model rocket for his sixth-grade science fair project. They took pictures of it in several stages of flight, from blastoff to ascent, parachute ejection, and touchdown. Scott's project won second prize that year. That day was second only to the red-letter day that Brent passed on his magnificent and greatly-coveted Matchbox car collection to Scott! They were good friends, but Brent moved out of Scott's realm before their brotherhood had really matured.

Because of the age difference, Brent began to seem more like a third parent and live-in babysitter, rather than the oldest child. Merryl read somewhere that more presidents, senators, and heads of corporations were first-born children than any others in the sibling order. *It seems more is expected of them,* she reflected, *and they're tougher 'cause they have to lead the way. They have to be the guinea pigs—the ones we new parents learn on. A doctor told me once that everyone thinks they've ruined their first born.*

After high school graduation, Brent took the initiative to get a security guard job and work out his junior college classes and the funding for them all by himself. He was the guy who spent his Christmas break condensing five huge computer manuals into one manageable operating manual so the junior college staff could implement their brand-new computer system. He was their fair-haired boy from then on and hired him as an instructor! He actually grew up to be the youngest officer of his bank in Rochester without the encouragement of a supportive father, without financial backing, without a college degree. (Lacking a required speech class was all that kept him from graduating.) Merryl felt she couldn't claim any credit for it. He decided to do it and did it, himself.

As Merryl absentmindedly stared out of the window of the bus, letting her mind wander without reins, the concrete speeding by blurred in her vision. The midsummer afternoon sun glared off the bright surface, reflecting a blinding whiteness into her eyes. As if triggered by the glare, a sense of utter aloneness inundated her. Her heart screamed out of her breast against the whiteness and the loneliness. The bus, the present, the intervening years dissolved and dropped her alone into the frightening whiteness.

I am alone, never before so alone — lost in this boundless vastness of white — everywhere cold, sterile, colorless, white linen. The gurney is covered with it, I am completely draped in it, and all the nurses, doctors, and orderlies are masked and impersonalized by it. The walls, the floor tiles, the ceiling are all white. I feel white inside—colorless, empty. Merryl remembered the scene. It seemed to materialize from the concrete. She was twenty but felt ten . . . or five. She seemed so small, but she knew she was having a baby. It all came charging at her with surrealistic clarity. *I have a husband and a mother somewhere, but they don't know that I am here. I just came in for tests to analyze my skyrocketing blood pressure. Now they tell me they have to take the baby before convulsions kill us both. I didn't think it would be like this. I thought Larry and I would come in together and this moment of destiny would be fun and exciting.*

But it's only lonely. No one seems to know my name. I'm not sure I have a name here. I'm a nonentity, suspended in the center of a white world, in a universe of nameless white. The color of my pale flesh against the sheets is the only sign of life. The large concentric circles of light above me are blinding white, bleaching away my life, reflecting on the cold, hard, stainless steel bars in dazzling, stabbing flashes of white. I'm an alien here. I feel disembodied from the familiar. It's so far away and lost to me. That injection is making me sick . . . so nauseated. I'm going to throw up on this impeccable white! Help me! Is there anybody here? The buzzer. Got to find that buzzer. Oh, God, I'm sick! I'm spinning in this whirling white! . . . A hand on my forehead, warm, firm. It feels kind. There are two eyes within that white . . . caring, compassionate eyes. There is life here, even here. As the anesthetic took effect and Merryl's consciousness was absorbed into the sea of white, her heart came to rest under the steady kindness of that saving hand.

Merryl's forehead bounced lightly against the window glass as the bus lurched to a stop. With confusion as she struggled to bring her being forward to the present, she tried to deny the tears filling her eyes and heart. They were coming with the force of a flashflood. Responding to an instinct to flee the onrush of emotion, Merryl thrust both her arms around the contents of her lap and lunged out the opening rear door of the bus. Alighting on the curb, she realized this wasn't her stop. She hadn't even thought about where she was, only of escape from the oncoming flood. As the bus moved on, Merryl sat down where she was on the tiny patch of grass between the sidewalk and the parking lot of the convenience store. The grass felt surprisingly cool through her hose. She let the few tears that would not be squelched seep through. With the tears came calm.

I will always thank God for the blessing of that hand. It brought peace to me when there seemed to be none. Merryl treasured the memory of the comforting touch that wrapped her cold body and soul in an aura of warmth as she disappeared from the realm of the living for two days. *I was never so small and so lost and so lonely as then, and God reached out to me through that hand to give me hope, pull me through. When I woke up, I was a mother.*

They kept her sedated for a full forty-eight hours until the threat of the toxemic convulsions was past. The pang of the pain that awakened her from the darkness of those two lost days came back to her with wincing sharpness. *That huge episiotomy was necessary, they said, in order to drag him into the world with forceps. I couldn't help; I was completely zonked. That little guy was so skinny—twenty-one inches long, but he looked like a little skeleton—hollow checks, spindly legs. He needed those extra two weeks till the due date to finish filling out. They snatched him into this world too soon. We got off to a bit of a bad start didn't we, Brent,* Merryl crooned to the newborn infant in her mind's eye.

Merryl reached in slow motion for a blade of grass as if grasping for a wisp of life, anything. Her fingers closed on the cool, living sliver of green. She let it pass slowly, deliciously through her fingers, enjoying its smooth freshness. *Life is wonderful,* she thought. *Brent's birth was not fun like the others', but it was wonderful just the same. Every baby is a miracle, even every blade of grass. The green glass beads are this color, the color of life, summer green. How my heart yearns for those beads.*

Merryl's eyes involuntarily lifted from the green of the blade of grass to the blue of the sky beyond the western trees. *God, you're still here, aren't you? Still here giving hope? Where else can I turn? You alone have the words of eternal life. Thank you for bringing Scott home. Help Bessie sort out the pieces of her broken heart in that hospital. Clue me in on how to keep up with Krista! Heal the rift between me and Brent. Show me how to help Larry find life worthwhile.*

Merryl watched her prayer arrows zinging heavenward. *I guess I send a zillion of those prayer arrows zinging every day,* she thought. A zillion zinging prayer arrows! The picture was intriguing. She visualized them skimming the tops of the trees, sailing over the river, through the white wisps of cloud, disappearing into the radiance of the sun. She followed them with the words of the psalmist, "Hear and answer me, oh God. Let my cry come unto you."

The second bus slowed as it passed as if to question why this woman was sitting pensively in the grass at the bus stop. For the first time, Merryl took stock of where she was. She had hopped off the bus at 36th Street instead of 43rd. She had a long walk ahead of her. She'd never waste a punch on her bus pass when she could walk. As she picked up her purse and the tote bag containing her walking shoes and the eye shadow kits, she noticed that she could see the Arkansas River from where she stood. Thirty-sixth Street ran straight into it just a couple of blocks ahead. Since she had several blocks to walk, it would be much more pleasant to walk the jogging trail along the river than to trudge the hot concrete along this busy street full of five o'clock traffic. Merryl felt delighted with the idea as she made the quick switch from her heels to her slip-on flats. Even though Merryl lived just two blocks from the riverpark, she spent little time there. There was always so much else to do. It would be a real treat to get away to the gravel trail that ran for seven or eight miles along the river's edge.

This unpredicted change in Merryl's routine seemed a little like an adventure. In the rush of this holiday-like spirit, she did what she considered a very frivolous thing. She stopped in at the Quik Trip store and plunked down fifty-two cents for a Dr. Pepper with ice to sip as she walked along. Pausing by the copy machine at the front of the store to affix the plastic snap-on lid to her paper cup and unwrap and insert the drinking straw through its hole, Merryl drew some of the cold, sparkling liquid up the straw into her eager mouth.

Ah, this is good! She felt like a kid. Reluctant to leave the air-conditioned convenience store for a long walk in Vulcan's furnace, Merryl hesitated at the plate glass window with the straw transfusing the refreshing liquid through her lips. The way the leaves of the small trees bordering the church across the street reflected the late-afternoon sun reminded her of the three Chinese elms that stood in front of the house on Columbia Avenue where she had grown up. Hot summer time was wonderful then.

This is just the kind of day we used to play in the hose. Oh, that was fun—darting back and forth through the sprinkler in our swim suits. Merryl could almost feel the cool, wet clover between her bare toes as she visualized those golden afternoons of splashing, laughing fun. How precious that memory felt. What a warm, secure, all's-well-with-the-world sensation went with it. The red-brick house with the white shutters and the big bay window that was in the background of all those memories of her childhood was her symbol of security, even yet.

I hope my kids have some good memories like that, Merryl thought. *They had fun that summer we got the Slip and Slide. They almost tore up the yard in their enthusiasm in sliding down the duplex terrace on that strip of wet, yellow plastic. They always had a wading pool of one kind or another, but it was almost always in a different yard each summer. We moved from job to job and rent house to rent house, never a house or memory that was really ours. I guess we did the best we could.* Merryl's vision blurred with the mist of a few rising tears as her eyes descended from the tree tops to the glaring concrete outside.

Snow! The out-of-focus sparkling concrete could have been snow. *It looked just like that in the parking lot lights from the hospital window.* Suddenly Merryl shivered. A chill coursed through her body, whether from the cold drink, the convenience store's air-conditioning, or the thought of that December night, she couldn't tell. She had stood at that window, just like this, in that darkened room while Brent was deciding between life and death. The Quik Trip window became the window of that room in the pediatric ward of St. Francis Hospital. The glaring white concrete was fresh, sparkling snow, bright in the lights of the almost empty hospital parking lot below. Merryl was there—transported back through time.

The snow had fallen softly all that day and night, making everything look clean and new from the hospital window, while Brent lay unconscious behind her with his incision gaping, tubes draining the killing poison from his abdomen. The doctor told her that fourteen was a susceptible age for the appendix to flare up. It seemed like the twenty-four-hour flu when Brent came home from school nauseated on Friday afternoon. But by Saturday morning, he was fine. He ate cold cereal and watched cartoons with the little kids. The doctor said that was the temporary relief after the inflamed appendix burst. By the time Merryl returned home from the grocery store Saturday evening, it was clear that something was not right; Brent felt weak and couldn't eat.

Sunday morning the family went to church without him. While kneeling in the little Catholic church, the white-hot explanation burst into Merryl's brain. It came like a laser beam, swift, sure, bright, unmistakable—one word: appendicitis. "I know what it is," she blurted out in a loud whisper to Larry next to her. "I know what it is!!" Nothing had ever hit her with that kind of clarity before. There could be no doubt of it. She couldn't wait to get home to call the doctor.

From her perspective of ten or so years, Merryl now realized how presumptuous she must have sounded telling that doctor on Sunday morning, "My son has appendicitis!" *He wouldn't believe me.* He said, from Brent's symptoms, he didn't think so. Of course, by then, the doctor figured out later, the appendix had already ruptured. *When I made the call, I planned to take Brent into the emergency room immediately, but the doctor insisted that we wait and bring him into his office on Monday morning. The doctor just wouldn't believe me. I told him it was appendicitis. If I told him that the Holy Spirit told me, he really would have thought I was nuts. It had to be the Holy Spirit; it just popped into my head. We should have gone straight to the hospital and not called at all.*

All day Sunday and all that night while waiting to go see the doctor, the poison seeped and spread through Brent's entire abdomen, corroding his tissues into peritonitis. He was delirious, hallucinating all Sunday night while that poison tried to destroy his healthy young body. By Monday morning Brent could not walk from the car into the clinic; they had to get a wheel chair for him. He couldn't even lift his arms when they tried to take the X-rays. They were sent immediately across the street to the hospital for emergency surgery. The doctor said the appendix had curved around and made a pocket to contain some of the pus, or it would have been much worse. When they cut him open, the doctor said the stench was so bad, he could hardly work over him. *It serves that doctor right. He should have believed me.*

The Merryl within Merryl turned from the sparkling blanket of snow crystals to the still figure lying in the room. The only light besides that reflected from the snow was coming from the equipment monitoring Brent's intravenous antibiotic drip. The doctor told her that just a few years earlier, before these high-powered antibiotics, he wouldn't have had a chance. The blinking red buttons of light and the green glowing numbers from the machine seemed to be mocking the ward's cheerful Christmas decorations in morbid imitation. The door opened slightly allowing the dimmed, late-night light from the hall to reveal the youthful face and tousled light brown hair of the unconscious patient.

"Everything OK?" the nurse whispered.

"I think so. He's quiet," was all Merryl knew to say.

"Well, let me know if you need anything." She softly disappeared. The nurses were tired. Most of them were working a second shift. The snow, beginning that morning while they were on their way to the doctor's office, kept on and on until Merryl couldn't get home, and the night shift nurses couldn't get in to relieve the ones on duty. As far as Merryl was concerned, she was glad to be stranded in this city within a city. There was no place else she wanted to be.

The nurse left the door open a crack, and Brent's face looked so young in the soft light. He was so innocent and child-like, reduced to helplessness there. He looked five again, only that time both his eyes were black and blue from the accident. She almost lost him then when the milk truck hit him right in their apartment driveway. After an emergency tourniquet, an ambulance ride, two plastic surgeries to repair a little arm they said was severed, he amazed them all. He was healthy and tough. *How many lives did this little guy have? Resiliency should be his middle name.*

Resiliency, resiliency. How her heart broke for him the day long ago in that California apartment when he turned away silently from his father's curt rebuff. *He wanted to ask me something, but Larry was talking to me and angrily refused him the chance to say a word. At five, Brent was already learning, like me, to swallow needs and feelings that we knew would find no sympathy. He slipped away without a sound, but I saw his little face as he turned the corner to go upstairs. It was contorted with soundless anguish. He was bawling without making one sound. Such hurt and pain, and he was absorbing it all into himself. What else could he do? Resilience. He began to learn it so young. Be resilient, Brent. Resiliency, remember? Fight! You can bounce back again.*

As Merryl approached the foot of his bed, her nostrils caught the putrid odor of the drainage from his open incision. The blanket was propped up on a frame over Brent's body to keep it from resting on the gaping wound she had glimpsed with horror as they moved him from the gurney into his bed. Merryl would never have believed a person could have a cavernous opening like that into the abdomen and be alive. The black hole, about four inches long and three inches wide, looked as if it went all the way through him. She couldn't understand why it wasn't bleeding.

The noodle-like tubes hanging out of it had to drain the foul, gangrenous pus from the cavity before it could be closed up. According to the doctor, that would take two or three weeks! That cavern would have to be irrigated with hydrogen peroxide every three hours night and day, even after he went home. Merryl had never smelled anything like the odor of that drainage. The orderlies placed deodorizers of several types in the room, but the rank smell of decomposing human tissue hung around the bed—the very stench of death. Its rotting, black insidiousness crawled up the nostrils, down into the stomach, hitting it with a sickening punch. The repellant odor required a physical and mental adjustment by the caretakers; to the mother, it was no impediment.

Merryl hovered in the room all evening after Brent came back from recovery. He didn't seem to be aware she was there, and there didn't seem to be anything she could do. There was a small couch provided where she could sleep, but for many hours, she alternated between standing at the window watching the drifting snow and standing by the bed watching her son's shallow breathing. He roused for only a few minutes as he came out of the anesthetic before the pain caused them to give him a sedative. Merryl was glad she was there for that moment of consciousness, but his despairing whispered words pierced her heart. "I think I'm dying . . . I think I want to die." His words of hopeless resignation were pervading the silent room. *Surely an almost-fourteen-year-old boy can't want to die*, Merryl screamed over and over inside of herself.

Standing at the end of the hospital bed, Merryl could see his bare feet under the blanket tent. She reached out to touch them. They were cold. She closed her hands around his cold, bare toes and began to gently, absent-mindedly massage the feet of her first born. "My, how these little toes have grown," Merryl mused aloud. He was a big boy, tall for his age, and very muscular from working out, but he was still just a boy inside. Only a few weeks before, he was crying himself to sleep when she slipped into his room to put his laundry away. Sitting on the edge of his bed, she stayed to listen to him talk about it. "I see other guys talking to their dads like they're such good friends, and it makes me feel so lonesome. There's a guy at the gym . . . sometimes his dad brings him dinner, and they sit and talk like buddies, and I just watch and think how great that must be to have a dad you can really talk to like that. You know, one who talks TO you, not AT you."

What could I say to him, except to let him know I understood. Before we were through talking, Larry was in the doorway criticizing and complaining that I needed to get to bed. I let him know I was big enough to decide when to go to bed, but it didn't help. What is it with him anyway that his heart is so small?

Merrylynn Cox

Now Merryl was pouring her love and compassion into those feet, stroking, caressing, massaging the circulation into them. "Live, Brent," she whispered. "You'll be fourteen day after tomorrow. Then comes Christmas in just ten more days. There's lots to live for. Please live, honey." *I'm sorry . . . I'm so sorry. I really love those green glass beads, really love them, really, really love them . . .*

Merryl was squishing her paper cup with a kneading motion that caused the snap-on lid to pop off and bring her back to the present and the Quik Trip window. *Oh, I've got to start walking. Dear God, I'm going to drive myself crazy,* thought Merryl as she robotically passed from the cool of the convenience store out into the afternoon heat.

Turning toward the river, Merryl noticed that the hot sun had dropped below the tops of the trees on the western bank, giving some welcome relief from its relentless pounding. Her thoughts turned toward home and the evening that awaited her there.

I'm so late, Krista will think I've fallen in a hole! I don't know what's for dinner. Oh darn! I should have bought milk at the Quik Trip. My mind's been like a sieve lately. What was it Mr. Shrum was saying at the bus stop yesterday? It was funny . . . He sure had a good idea today about bottling some of this weather for winter! Oh yes, I remember. Yesterday he was saying, there are three signs of early senility. "The first one is forgetfulness . . . and I can't remember the other two!" That's me, senility setting in along with the gray hairs. I've got to get some laundry done tonight, oh yes, and see if I have some paper to wrap Tami's present in. I ought to bake a cake or something for Scotty to welcome him home. I wish I'd been there to talk to him. Hope things will be better this time. I wonder if his eyebrows have grown back.

Merryl seemed to live her life around her children's lives, but what mother didn't? For all this emancipated talk about careers and fulfillment, she never met a mother who would rather work than take care of her kids. She had read about such career women, but all the working mothers she knew of were working strictly from hunger. Who would take on an additional forty hours' work a week for fulfillment? The main job was always there waiting when she got home. Fulfillment to her was taking care of her home and family. The job was just an interference. *Needing money is such a nuisance,* she decided. And the frequent stress migraines that plagued her were no help.

The walk along the river was pleasant. The Riverpark Commission had turned the smelly old river into a city asset. Merryl hadn't been to the riverpark, just two blocks from her house, since the Fourth of July fireworks display a month earlier. *I really ought to get over here more often,* she thought with enthusiasm. The joggers were out on the trail in full force, disregarding the heat. Merryl loved to read their T-shirts. Some were priceless. *There's a great one.* The white letters stood out against the sweaty navy shirt as it loped past: Work is for people who don't know how to fish. *Well! That must be where I made my big mistake—I learned to type instead of to fish!* Merryl concluded as she walked and meditated on T-shirt philosophy.

Swinging her jacket like the happy wanderer, Merryl felt as if she'd had a mini vacation by the time she turned the corner to her street. She could see her driveway halfway down the long block. Good, the old Volkswagen was gone.

That meant Larry had already gone to work for the night. Their good car, the Ford Lynx, had been repossessed last spring after Larry walked off his job for some still vague reason, and they were sharing the old blue bug Brent left behind.

She tried not to judge Larry too severely; Merryl had walked off a job without notice herself once. It was when they were in California and couldn't find a decent babysitter for Brent. How they came to be way out there is another story. Larry left her in the lurch. She learned he actually gave notice on his artist's job at the Tulsa neon sign shop that time and had been planning his secret departure for two weeks! Instead of picking up Brent and getting her at work as he promised on that winter day, he had packed the old Chevy and taken off toward the Western horizon. After an hour of fruitless waiting for him at work, she got a ride to the day nursery and home to find his goodbye note in the dark duplex. With no word from him for several weeks, he just turned up again on their doorstep. He insisted on putting all their meager earthly possessions in a U-Haul and doing the California-or-Bust thing, leaving everything familiar behind. *What a saga!* He hoed strawberries with the itinerants until he got a commercial art job at Prescolite in San Leandro. She car-pooled to the hills of Coyote from San Jose to work as a secretary at United Technology Center, making solid rocket fuel for the Titan II. *That lasted for a couple of years until our California girl, Bessie, was born. A short-lived job offer for Larry in Tulsa brought us back when she was only a few weeks old, back to more unemployment, a suicide attempt, the psyche center and adultery.*

The front stoop of her house coming into view placed

Merryl squarely back into her real world. She never knew what to expect when she rounded the corner in the evening. She had come home to some awful messes. She found arguments raging between father and son with a red-light-flashing police car at the scene, summoned by neighbors. There was more than one instance of finding more or less wholesale destruction when she opened the front door—pieces of lamps, furniture, and bric a brac from wall to wall, scattered by the unhappy lord and master. There were two more half-hearted suicide attempts by him in the past year or so. The last weird "cry for help" so unnerved her that she refused to bring her husband home from the hospital or live with him for several months after that. He had doused himself with gasoline, set himself on fire, then chickened out and jumped into the river's sewage plant reservoir! That bizarre incident actually made the newspapers! But, as always, in time she gave in again—soft in the heart or soft in the head—a glutton for punishment.

When she was sure Larry wasn't going to be home in the evening, her world took on a sense of peace. It was only at those times that Merryl realized how she tiptoed through their relationship at the other times. It was no wonder. The tension had a way of erupting in her face in the most unexpected ways. It didn't do any good to ask herself, "What did I do; what did I say to make him so mad?" There didn't usually seem to be an easily identifiable connection.

That other rent house bedroom door probably still bore the scar of the wooden toy rifle butt that eleven-year-old Brent wielded against it when he came to her rescue once. He received the worst of it for his protective instincts. Krista was born in that bedroom with a midnight birthday cake to greet her arrival! After two in-hospital natural deliveries with Lisabeth and Scotty, Merryl had enough confidence in the birth process that she was sure she could do it herself with the help of a midwife. Everyone had protested, but Merryl reminded the objectors that both her parents were born at home. She had to try to undo the completely sterile experience of Brent's birth.

She wanted to buy that house and had the chance to. That was her favorite house of all their little rent houses, and they lived there longer than any of the others. She left a big part of her heart there when it was sold out from under them. Larry always said he didn't want the responsibility of owning a house. He said he especially didn't want to buy that one because it held so many bad memories of Brent's tumultuous high school years. There was always some excuse or another for not owning their own home.

Merryl wasn't the only object of Larry's hair-trigger temper. He and Brent had come to physical blows several times. The only family vacation they ever took, to a cabin on Flint Creek near Siloam Springs for a week, was spoiled and cut short by a violent outburst of their mutual antagonism. When Scott, the second son, was in grade school, he made a decision as he witnessed those fearsome fights: It would never happen to him. In later years, whenever his dad threatened him with physical force, Scott went limp as a rag. He ended the fight before it began and kept all his hostility inside. Merryl thought it was taking the greater toll on him because of that. Brent always let it come out in some way. But that wasn't good either.

The sisters at St. Agnes' School in Springfield, when Larry worked for the ad agency, were concerned about Brent when he violently scribbled up his second-grade textbooks. They called the parents in for a series of counseling sessions with a psychologist. *I don't remember his name, but he was a great guy. He pinpointed the problem right away—Brent's trouble was his parents. That made me feel just great! We never discussed Brent again, only us. He said one thing to me I have never forgotten. Sensing my feelings of inadequacy, he told me, "I'd be glad to have you for my mother." "Really?" I answered with genuine astonishment. I thought to myself, He doesn't know how awful I am. Who would want me for a mother? But it made me begin to look at myself a little differently and think maybe Brent could love me. I found it so hard to believe he could.*

Merryl knew she lacked confidence in her instincts as a mother. She was naturally easy going and allowed her kids plenty of freedom—maybe too much. They could talk her in or out of almost anything, especially since Brent's high school graduation. She was so adamant that night about his wearing a collared shirt and a tie with his cap and gown that he roared away from the house in his VW, refusing to even attend his graduation ceremony. She had been sorry about it ever since. Maybe she made too big a deal about it. Maybe traditions like that weren't really that important any more. Anyway, the cost was too high, so she no longer pressed insignificant points like that. She knew her kids had to be allowed to grow up by making some of their own decisions—and mistakes.

That was Larry's trouble—he had never been allowed to grow up. Perhaps that's why he found adulthood so frightening. He never had a long enough tether from his mom's over-protection to make any mistakes or develop any independence. Larry described his growing-up experience as being akin to a plant trying to grow in a dark basement under a bell jar. He was never allowed to be a Cub Scout or have a paper route or play in another boy's yard or even ride his bike, except for the few feet in front of his own house between his driveway and the driveway next door. Merryl read in a psychology magazine that over-protection is the most severe form of abuse, because it tells a child he can't do anything right. It took Merryl many years to realize that Larry's self-image was even worse than her own.

What a pair of misfits they made. They seemed so well-matched when their relationship started in their high school year book staff art class. Two artistic starry-eyed loners! But so naïve and not ready for married life. That first double date picnic with Bill and Loretta, artist friends from high school, should have clued her in that this guy was poison – she came home with a horrible case of poison ivy! Nevertheless, they enrolled in college together as art majors, but Merryl had to drop out right after their wedding in the middle of their second year to go to work, so he could continue. Brent arrived barely eleven months later! What an unstable situation to be born into! Someone could make a good case here that some people really shouldn't be allowed to have children. How much damage had they done by their immaturity to those precious human beings entrusted to their care?

A panorama of remembered violent scenes passed before Merryl's eyes. She tried to view them from a child's perspective. Bessie, a child herself, cuddled and protected the younger two during those loud rages. There were so many instances of crashing crockery and holes put in walls in their presence. She knew her children must have some terrifying memories, like Larry's earliest ones of hiding in the dark, listening to his parents scream and slug it out. Merryl never had the courage to fight back in those battles like Larry's Cherokee Indian mother did. She simply did her best to protect herself.

Merryl was never hurt badly enough in those periodic holocausts to require treatment—just badly enough to lie low for a few days while a black eye, a sprained ankle, or a few cuts and bruises healed. She spent those days silently cursing him with every aching movement but had stuck it out, counting on a transformation miracle—for twenty-seven years now. *God, do you realize that's longer than Abraham waited for Isaac? That's twice as long as Joseph waited for his release from slavery and prison. Do I have to wait as long as Israel waited for the Messiah? I'm tired of waiting.*

Merryl's mini vacation had already worn off by the time she climbed the three steps of her porch. The front door was wide open. The window fan was going full blast, doing its best to make the living room bearable. Merryl left strict rules that the air conditioners were not to be turned on when Larry wasn't home. The cool air helped him remain calm, but the rest of them could do without them very well, and running them was just too expensive.

"Where've you been?" Krista stuck her head around from the kitchen. "I was getting worried! You always tell me to call when I'm going to be late."

"I know," sighed Merryl. "I'm sorry. I just missed the bus." It seemed the simplest explanation.

"I found some fish sticks and some frozen French fries. I was starved, so I stuck 'em in the oven. They're almost ready."

"Great," said Merryl approvingly, glad not to have to bother with dinner. Merryl's youngest was a brand-new teenager and was getting quite capable when she wanted to be. "Open a can of those green beans, why don't you. And could you pour me a glass of that sun tea in the refrigerator?"

"O.K.," was the cheerful, welcome reply. Flinging her purse, jacket, and bag on the couch, Merryl sank into the red rocker directly in front of the window fan. She kicked her shoes into the air and closed her eyes as she wiggled her hot toes in the artificial breeze. She had rocked four babies in that old platform rocker. It was a gift from Larry's Aunt Madie, purchased at a close-out sale, to welcome Brent into the world. Merryl had re-covered it twice; it hadn't been red for years, but it would always be the "red rocker" to her.

The clinking of ice cubes enticed her attention from her cooling toes. "What didja get for Tami?" Krista momentarily interrupted the breeze to hand her the glass of tea.

"Thanks, hon. You're an angel of mercy! It's in my bag on the couch. Oh, just a minute." She remembered the duplicate eye shadow gifts that were to be future surprises for her girls. "Hand me my bag, and I'll show you." Merryl carefully extracted the little gift without exposing the others and handed it to Krista with a "ta da!" flourish.

"Hey, that's neat! I want one!"

"I knew you'd say that, but it's not your birthday!"

The stove timer dinged, and soon Merryl received a plate of food from Krista's hands without having to budge. *This is the life,* thought Merryl, *for one brief, shining moment . . . till laundry.*

Krista sat across from Merryl on the couch to keep her company and, also, because it was much cooler in the living room than in the kitchen. She chatted as she dipped her French fries in a spreading pool of ketchup on her plate.

"Seems funny to be just me and you, doesn't it? I miss Scotty and Bessie, don't you?"

"Sure do, honey!"

"When I was babysitting this afternoon, I saw this thing on T.V. about the Middle Ages, like that class Bessie took last semester, remember? It was kinda boring, but there wasn't anything else on but a really ancient cowboy movie and that dumb cooking show. Bessie sure was right when she told us that was a real churchy time. Boy, those guys back then were holy. I mean, they didn't know much about science or anything, but they were really into God and all that stuff. Everything they did was about God. Everything they wrote or painted was about saints or Mary and Jesus and Bible stuff. And you know what? They were so holy and thought God was so important and they were so unimportant that a lot of those monk guys didn't even sign their names to their paintings or statues they made. They just wrote 'For the glory of God,' and nobody even knows who made them. Can you imagine? They got their kicks out of sitting around 'saying their beads.' Do you know what that means? . . . saying prayers, like on a rosary, you know. I guess 'beads' means prayers . . ."

Krista's voice droned on in the waning heat of the afternoon. Merryl had stopped listening on that phrase "beads means prayers" . . . "beads means prayers" . . . "green glass beads means prayers." The string of green glass beads lay before her in the air. They looked more beautiful to her than ever. They had become larger than life, and the series of brilliant emerald-green beads on their string lay in a hauntingly graceful curve. From the tiny beads on the far ends, they became progressively larger as they loomed toward her and the center of the length of string. The larger, nearer beads shimmered with an inner iridescence that diffused around them as a soft glow. The beauty of the phantom beads obsessed her. Merryl's chest swelled with such a desperate craving, yearning for the lost beads that she could hardly bear it. *Where are you? Where have you gone? What has become of you? Can't I ever have you back?*

"Beads means prayers." It was a voice from an unplumbed depth. *What? . . . What is that?"* she thought. *"Beads . . . means . . . prayers."*

"Mom, are you asleep? You're about to spill your French fries!"

"Oh, . . . I guess I'm tired . . . I've had enough. Do you want the rest?"

"Sure!"

"I've got to change my clothes and start the laundry."

In the bedroom, Merryl laid her pink blouse on the bed while she hung up her old gray suit. Turning back toward the bed, she stood for a moment in her slip to privately indulge herself in the blessing of that aurora shade one more time. She reached to finger the ties with heartfelt appreciation. *Thank you, pretty pink. You helped me make it through the day. You're a Valentine from me to me. What better time for a Valentine than August?* Somehow that still seemed shamefully selfish, but she was quick to spring to her own defense. *Someone said something once about 'If not me, who; if not now, when?' I'm pretty sure they weren't talking about pink blouses, but it doesn't hurt for me to be a little nice to me once in a while.* Merryl felt justified as she slipped on her light wrap-around dress and sandals.

It was time to tackle laundry logistics again. While

loading towels into the washing machine, Merryl began the mental gyrations of her drying plan. She could hang the pants and button shirts on hangers on the shower rail, the lingerie on the towel tree. She could hook some of the T-shirts on hangers on the kitchen doorframe and some on the cabinet door handles. She'd have to wait and hang the heavy jeans, towels, and sheets on the line outside in the morning. Merryl was far too tight to waste seventy-five cents a load drying her clothes at the laundromat when she could get around it with a little bit of inconvenience. Her resourcefulness worked pretty well if you didn't object to damp laundry in your face when you passed through a doorway or took a bath.

As the load of towels churned, Merryl leaned on the vibrating washing machine, studying the useless empty shell of the dryer next to it. *Just one more complication of my ridiculous life . . . who would believe it?* A one-armed bandit, the real thing, had stolen the insides of her dryer. She tried to help out the one-armed man when he knocked on her door looking for odd jobs. He said he'd fix it cheap. She even gave him money to buy the parts. He took the entire heating unit out and then held it hostage, trying to charge her fifty dollars to get it back. The police called it a domestic matter and said they couldn't help her. Oh well, she concluded, she was no worse off with an empty-shell dryer than a broken one. Merryl had long ago given up watching soap operas. They seemed so dull and contrived, compared to her own life.

While Merryl was separating lights and darks, the phone rang . . . and rang . . . and rang. "Krista, are you going to get that?"

From her bedroom, Krista answered nonchalantly, "I thought you were going to get it."

"Krista, I'm in the laundry room. Could you get the phone, please, before they hang up?"

"Jimmi-n-e-e-e! I have to do everything around here."

"You poor dear!" muttered Merryl. "She knows it's going to be for her anyway."

In a minute Krista came to the laundry room door. "Did you find me some birthday paper?"

"I haven't looked yet, but I will. It's right up there on that shelf."

"I can't reach it."

"Well, just give me a few minutes, and I'll get it."

"Oh, Bessie's on the phone."

"Well, for Goodness' sake, why didn't you say so?" Merryl sputtered as she scrambled over the piles of laundry and up the steps to the kitchen.

"Wee Bess!" Merryl gleefully exclaimed into the phone. Her daughter would be twenty in a couple of months, but the baby nickname still came out affectionately from time to time. Her name was really Lisabeth, but as a toddler, she couldn't say it and had called herself "Wee Bess." It stuck, and as she grew, it became simply Bess. "I didn't think they'd let you call me."

"Well, I guess I'm sort of a trustee, now. They've decided I have a chance of returning to the normal world, at least for short periods. They said I could come home for a couple of hours tonight if you'd come and sign me out and get me back by ten."

"Oh, sweetheart, how I'd love to, but Daddy has the car. He's gone clear to Owasso. He got a temporary job waxing floors in a discount store. He hates it, but at least he's working. I'm sorry. I'd love to see you."

"Oh . . ."

Merryl had the feeling the disappointed voice was going to cry. "But we can talk on the phone, can't we?" Merryl offered quickly, brightly.

"I guess so. I just miss you so much."

"I miss you, too, darlin'. How's it going?"

"O.K., I guess, but some of these people are weird!"

"Well, honey, that is a psychiatric unit."

"Yeah, I know, but next to some of them, I look like Miss Stability of the Universe!" Merryl laughed. How good it felt to laugh. When was the last time she had laughed a real laugh?

Of all the children, Lisabeth was the most like her father. She was the most sensitive to mood swings and extremes. As a baby, she always reacted to every new face or situation with intense delight or traumatic tears. Before she was two, Merryl dubbed her "my Sarah Bernhardt" and prayed for Heaven's help in Wee Bess's first love affair. Her emotionality was a great asset in high school drama class—she received the only "A" — but in real life, it could be a handicap. As her daughter described some of the inexplicable antics of the inmates of the unit, Merryl listened with half an ear. She was preoccupied with heavier matters.

I thought she was going to kill herself over that dumb boy. He was never the most macho, but homosexual . . .! Who would have thought . . .? What a crazy world this has turned out to be. I ache for the way it was. Life seemed so much simpler and cozier when the kids were little. But it was rough then, too. Why don't I ever get used to it?

Bessie was saying something important. "I've been doing a lot of thinking and writing about everything. It's amazing how much time there is in a week when there's nothing else to do. I really am going to be O.K. I thought Eric really loved me, and I don't know how he could have gone off with some guy when we were practically engaged, but now I realize he's got a long, hard road ahead of him, and it was really nothing to do with me. I'm O.K., really. They've helped me, Mom. I've been really praying for Eric, and I feel better. I've learned some things. I know there's joy even in the pain of loving. It's as if the pain digs a well of black emptiness deep into the soul until it taps a small spring that becomes a soothing, forgiving fountain. You can only find the spring by allowing the pain to dig through, but then the spring and the fountain soothe the abrasion of the pain. I know now, love is never wasted. No matter where it ends up, how it gets used up or abused, it's never lost. We're always better for it when love passes through us. Love blesses coming or going. It's never wasted."

Merryl was stunned. She sat silent, absorbing the wisdom of the ages coming through her daughter. The childcare manual was right. She had copied the entire chapter on the Difficult Child for Lisabeth's baby book. It was such an exact description of her. It said that if the terrible twos could be survived with this type of child, he or she would grow up into the most enthusiastic, most delightful, most giving, loving person of all.

"Mom? . . . Are you there?"

"Yes, honey, I'm here. I'm just kind of overwhelmed. I've had a rough day, and that was just what I needed to hear."

"Well, I can't talk on this phone long. I have to get off now, but I'll get to come home in a few days. I'll let you know when. Love you. Bye."

"Bye, Bessie . . . Oh, Bessie . . . I didn't tell her about Scotty. She would have been glad."

Merryl wandered back to the laundry room, knowing there was something she hadn't finished but not being able to remember what it was. Her heart was experiencing a strange tingly sensation, as if the circulation was returning after a long absence. She held her breath as she examined the sensation with wonder. *That's joy*, she thought with amazement. *I can still feel joy!*

Merryl remembered that old feeling of joy from her ballet days! Those were the days that brought her to feeling more like a sister to Bessie than a mother. They were ballet buddies all through her elementary school and junior high. *I had ballet in my blood from my growing-up years. It was always my favorite thing to do. The highlight joy of my life was performing in the classic white ballets, Swan Lake and Giselle with the Civic Ballet. I did so want Bessie to have that love of ballet, too.* Merryl had to earn their lessons by being the ballet school's secretary in the evenings, answering the phone and keeping attendance records. She even spent her Saturdays for a while caring for their teacher's aging mother, who just happened to have been Merryl's very first beloved ballet teacher. But all the time that mother and daughter spent coming and going to classes together bonded them into sisterhood. Those were years of joy! Even though Larry was never sympathetic (his mantra was "Babies and ballet, that's all you care about, babies and ballet!"), ballet was salve to so many of the daily traumas.

The washing machine was beginning the first spin cycle, draining out the soapy water for the rinse, and Merryl remembered what it was she had been doing. She filled the plastic baskets with the separated light and dark piles of dirty clothes. While she was waiting for the rinse cycle and time to add the fabric softener to the towels, Merryl decided she'd look on the laundry room shelf for the birthday paper for Tami's present. Merryl had been trained by her Scotch mama, married during the Great Depression, to pick up pennies she found, to scrape mayonnaise jars and butter cube wrappers for every last smidgen, and to save all the hand-me-downs and every scrap of gift wrap. This extreme economizing was in Merryl's blood, too, and even though her husband and kids ridiculed it all the time, her "making do and doing without," to use Larry's derogatory words, had produced many meals and outfits out of little more than her imagination.

As Merryl leafed through the pieces of paper in the big gift wrap box, she realized some of them were genuine relics. She noticed one saved from her very first baby shower. She'd had many opportunities to use it again over the years, but the little round pink and blue babies were so cute and held such precious memories, she just kept it at the bottom of the box until it became quite yellowed with age. Many of the saved pieces were becoming too small from many uses and cuttings to be much good for anything, but she kept them because someday she might need one for a little eye shadow kit for Tami's birthday—and here was the very scrap—tiny red hearts and blue teddy bears. *Perfect!*

"What's this?" Merryl's heart skipped a beat as she inadvertently turned up a corner of a large piece of wrapping paper that was carefully folded inside out. It was a blue foil Christmas design with white doves in the middle of silver wreaths. She remembered opening that package. It must have been six or seven years before. It was the most special package of her whole life. *How old was Brent then? Nineteen probably. Married and divorced already.* It lasted only five months. Married right out of high school. They tried to talk him out of it, but he always was so sure of what he wanted. That had been the trouble. He and Sherry talked about college, but he meant it, and she hadn't. He wouldn't settle for working as a foreman in her daddy's plant. Brent had been forceful about it and that had ended it, and it almost ended him. He went down through hell over that divorce. He came back home to live with them for a while before he left town for good. *How I ached for him when he took their wedding picture out in the back yard and held a lighted match to it. It was as if his heart went up in smoke. He never shared his pain. He was so used to carrying it alone and silently.*

Merryl smoothed the shimmering paper laid out on top of the washing machine. That day . . . that Christmas day . . . was the day he told her he had decided long before, on that garage sale afternoon, that he was never going to give her another present. Merryl was inundated by the memory of when he told her of his six-year-old decision for a life-long moratorium on gifts. She always knew it but had never faced it directly. She couldn't face a wound so deep, not when she caused it. She visualized it as that ugly appendix wound, only bigger, deeper, bloodier, and smellier, oozing the pus of hurt and unforgiveness toward her.

That's why that Christmas gift had meant so much to her. It was sacred. It was more than a beautiful full-length wine velour bathrobe with embroidered pink roses on the lapels; to her it was a healing offering of a broken heart. "My sacrifice is this broken spirit. You will not scorn this crushed and broken heart," King David said. She knew that since his divorce, Brent's heart had become mushy with pain and regret, and he, like David, had been reaching out to God again for healing . . . love. During those high school years, Brent put God on a shelf, saying, "Don't bug me, God; I'll be back." He had long since come back to God, and now Merryl felt the bridge being restored between herself and her son and his trust again in Love that this bathrobe represented. That bridge had never been torn down between them, but there were some huge holes in it that made passage back and forth across it difficult and dangerous. With the large Christmas box open on her lap, she sensed repair work in progress.

Merryl knew the bathrobe must have been very expensive and taken a large chunk of his small, part-time security guard check. She was acutely aware of the sacrifice he had made for her and felt uncomfortable in the awesome scope of the moment. It was so unexpected, like the moment of the offering of the beads. What could she do; what could she possibly say that could convey what she understood, that she knew what this meant? She thanked him warmly from across a room littered with boxes, bows, and wrapping paper. She attempted to express her awareness of the value of his gift as best she could with clumsy, human words. It had become difficult to hug him. She'd have to find a way today.

Brent grinned from across the room with awkward acknowledgment of her pleasure. To everyone else in the room, the box contained a lovely bathrobe. To Merryl, and surely to Brent, it was something more. "Look in the bottom," Brent said teasingly. Startled, Merryl turned her interest from the embroidered roses to rummaging among the voluminous velour folds and tissue paper in the box on her lap. There was another box, small, narrow, and silver—the kind that jewelry comes in. Merryl removed the lid carefully. On the cotton lay a sparking gold chain for her neck. Anyone could see that it was real gold from the dazzling brilliance with which it caught and reflected the colors of the Christmas tree lights. Merryl had never owned anything that was real gold except her wedding ring.

She fastened the spring clasp behind her neck as she stood up to look in the oval mirror above the desk behind her. The chain encircled the base of her throat like a filament of sunshine. It would never be her green beads, but it was close. She touched it to see if it was a mirage like the beads had become. It felt firm and solid and lasting. She had a sudden fleeting visual image of treasure chests at the bottom of the sea, spilling gold, undamaged after centuries, and of golden Inca ornaments, discovered in ruins, still bright and beautiful after a thousand years. *This is forever,* Merryl's spirit stated emphatically.

Beaming, she turned to her little son. His body may have been nineteen years old, but that morning he was six. She went to him through the clutter of bright paper. She stooped to put her arms around him the way she had so often imagined she had done on that summer day so long ago. She felt his light brown hair against her cheek. She turned to kiss it and hugged him again as she whispered in his ear, "Thank you." Could he understand what she was saying? *Brent, we are living that day over again. There is no time in His Spirit. We can go back there together and do it again and do it right. Can I hope you understand?"

The tears were falling on the blue foil paper. The tears she had been fighting back all day came freely, splashing on the doves and silver wreaths. *Did he understand? Can he ever understand and forgive me?"* she sobbed.

The washing machine went completely through the rinse cycle, and Merryl never added the fabric softener. Somehow that slip-up took on grand proportions in her somber mood as symbolic of her general ineffectiveness. She couldn't seem to help her children; she wasn't able to make her husband happy. He was definitely under the circumstances these days, and so she was too. She could overcome all the world but his constant depression. How could she help her sons rise above that oppressive pall if she wasn't able to manage it herself? Brent moved as far away from it as he could after that last outlandish display of his dad's antagonism toward him when Larry angrily tossed their only T.V. out the front door after him, trashing it on the driveway. Evidently Scott, the docile one, was ready to try living with his dad again. Merryl could empathize with what must be Scott's very mixed emotions of eagerness and trepidation as he returned home. She felt it every time Larry entered the house.

Bessie seemed to understand her daddy better than anyone but still found that being so much like him made it no easier to be around him, especially this summer when she was suffering so much turmoil of her own. That college scholarship was a double boon to her, providing her an education and distance from the home situation as well. Krista was the one who saw everything so matter of factly. "Blow him off, Mom," was her solution. She didn't yet understand the bonds of twenty-seven years of marriage and four children. "I'll never put up with that kind of crap," she insisted, and Merryl was sure she wouldn't. She was of a new generation of independent womanhood.

Merryl knew she was old fashioned. She was committed and loyal to her marriage to a fault. It was partly her Catholic upbringing and partly the great American family ideal of the Fifties that had formed her, but mainly it was a choice to believe God. She believed that she and her husband became one flesh in marriage till death would part them. The trouble was that she had begun wishing from time to time that death <u>would</u> part them. At times she even felt she would be glad to be the one to volunteer to depart if her kids could get along without her.

"Love never fails," the street preacher reminded her. She had always wanted to hold onto that. She wanted with her entire substance to believe it. Why wasn't it working? She must be doing everything wrong. She tried to love. Maybe she didn't know how. She tried to learn to follow the description of love in the Bible—patient, kind, long-suffering, bearing, enduring, and hoping all things. It seemed that all she was really learning was what she could do without— good cars, T.V.'s, dryers, financial stability . . . and even . . . love.

The house was beginning to look like a tenement alley with laundry drying everywhere. Krista went to bed after wrapping the birthday present and making plans on the phone with Tami for an hour for the upcoming slumber party. She had to babysit again early on Saturday for the lady who gave the swimming lessons. It was chapel quiet in the house as Merryl set beside the back door the heavy basket of wet towels, sheets, and jeans to be hung out on the clothesline in the morning. The window fan, valiantly drawing in the cooler night air, was the only other thing still working at this late hour as far as she knew, except for poor Larry. She pictured him swinging that mop over that huge discount store floor in Owasso. *Poor guy. Of course he's miserable. Who wouldn't be, having to do that all night, all alone?* Her heart reached out to him, wanting to ease his misery. *He thinks I don't care. I do care, but complaining won't help.* It was Merryl's philosophy—if it won't help, don't do it. She figured as long as she was stuck with life, she might as well make the best of it. Old Marcus Aurelius had understood: "Very little is needed for a happy life; it is all within you, in your way of thinking." Merryl said a heartfelt *"Amen, brother!"* to his ancient wisdom. The only answer, Merryl was sure, was to keep on believing that Love can't fail.

The phone ringing in the silence made Merryl jump. "Hello?" she whispered into the receiver.

"Mom?"

Who could be calling her "Mom" at this hour she thought? Scott was on a bus heading this way; this was definitely a male voice. "Brent?" He hadn't called her from Rochester in months.

"Your phone's been busy every time I've tried it tonight. I just wanted to thank you for the tricycle."

"What?"

"The tricycle you gave me when I was about Broch's age . . . I just wanted to thank you for it, in case I never had."

Merryl didn't know what to say. "Well . . . well, you're welcome. Whatever made you think of such a thing?"

"We gave Broch his first tricycle today, and it made me remember my big green trike and how much I loved it. I didn't know if I ever told you thanks."

This is my little boy, mused Merryl, *and he will always be my little boy for as long as he calls me "Mom." What a big little boy he has become, now with a wife and a little boy of his own.* Lisa was a gift of God for Brent. She was a student of his when he taught computer science at the junior college. It seems they went out for coffee one evening and decided to get married. Now they had four-year-old Broch, and Brent was a model father. When the new grandparents and young aunts and uncle met baby Broch, Brent's brother and sisters were shocked at his fatherly attentiveness. "Mom, I think Brent likes him," Krista observed in disbelief. The last image they had of their big brother was that of the merciless tease.

"Remember the big, red wooden blocks you had to rubber-band to the pedals to make them reach my feet? We had to do the same thing for Broch. It really took me back there and made me appreciate what you did for me. I remember it so well. That trike meant so much to me, and I was so glad to be able to do the same thing for Broch and make him as happy as you made me. We had a great time today. I just really want to say thanks."

"Oh, Brent," Merryl was listening in breath-held rapture. What could she say to convey her gratitude for this son's recognition of his mother's love? The trite, formal, "It was my pleasure," burst forth from her heart with all the sincerity the words could possibly contain. "You can't know how this touches me. I've been thinking about you all day long. I've been thinking about when your appendix ruptured and about the wonderful invention conglomerations you used to make and about . . . and about . . . about the beads you bought me at the garage sale . . . when you were six . . . those green glass beads."

"I remember . . ."

"Oh, Brent, I broke your heart that day. I'm so sorry. I never have been able to believe I could have done it. It's been haunting me. I want to do that day over again so badly. I'm so sorry about it. I just can't forgive myself. Did you hate me? Did you have any idea how I was suffering that day? Did you have any idea . . . of what was going on with me and Dad?"

"No . . . I was so little. I didn't understand anything except I knew I was hurt . . . and didn't know why. I remember, when I saw those green beads, I wanted to buy them for you so much. I remember trying so hard to get together enough money before somebody else bought them, and I was so happy to finally get them for you and didn't understand why you didn't want them. I just remember feeling cut off and sad."

"I'm so sorry I made you feel like that. I can't stand knowing I hurt you. I needed love so much then, and there you were, offering me so much, and I thoughtlessly spurned it. I don't know how I could ever have been so cruel. Did you ever forgive me?"

"I grew up. It's O.K. I learned what life is about. I've learned it's harder to forgive yourself than it is to forgive other people. I've done more than forgive you. I've found out what it feels like to crush a heart that loves and trusts you. Being a father now, I've had the same kind of thing happen. Not long ago, Broch and I were watching T.V. together on the couch. He did a flip-flop turnaround to hop down and somehow kicked me in the lip with his shoe. It surprised me and hurt, and I lashed out at him and called him stupid. It killed me to see the way that word socked the very life out of him. It was as if I had bashed him. He was so wounded it was like he was physically bruised. I never realized the effect my words could have on him. I didn't mean to hurt him so. I felt awful."

"Then you can understand?"

"Now I can. I know you loved me. You just always did. Remember that night in the hospital after they took my appendix out? . . . I knew it was my decision whether I was going to live or die. I just somehow knew I could go or stay. It was just knowing you were there that made me stay. I remember being aware you were there. I remember thinking, 'She loves me,' without even thinking of what that means; 'she just loves me, and it's enough. I could let go, but that's enough. It's all taken care of. I have what I need. I'll stay.' I even wrote a sorta poem about that a while back. I've been thinking about doing that for years. I was going to send it to you some time. Hold on. I'll get it."

Can this be happening? thought Merryl. She was giddy with the release of something like swirling bubbles in her brain.

"Here it is. I called it 'It Hurts So Little.' You know I'm not a poet . . . It's not much. It's just the way I felt.

Sleeping here with my gut cut open and draining, I feel very weak.
A gentle breeze of a thought rolls toward me.
It's not dark; there's no foreboding: It's up to you; will you live or come home?
Your next breath is your choice.

In my unconsciousness my spirit reasons: What's to keep me here?
My life's so violent. I don't like myself, and I'm all alone.

But I think my mother is sleeping on the cushions beside me.
She's different.

I can't see her problems. She's tried to discuss them with me,

But even if I get up on my tip toes, I can't understand.
All I see is what I need. I don't have to understand my need, but
     I can see.

Is there a word? No, I'm too young for words.
I'm still not convinced they're necessary; I seem to get by fine
     without them.

But what is it? I think it's love. Now, in my state, the excitement
     of life is quiet.
I have a question to answer: Is love enough?

Something inside me is certain; no thought's required.
I'm not thinking about pain, past or present.
She loves me. See. See. Here and there, she loved me.

I'm stable. I can see! See, that's love!
I feel it now, but the feeling comes from seeing,
Seeing other's actions spell LOVE.

My needs weren't GREAT. They were small.
But I've seen love, and that's met them all.

Yes, I'll stay; save heaven for another day.
If there's love here, I'll stay; IT will make a way.

I'm well now, and older. The world's excited again—much
     more so.

Jesus, I understand that you didn't make a sound as they nailed
     you to the cross. Had you seen love? I guess it was enough
     for you too.

A profound quiet had settled on the world. Peace was everywhere across the breadth of eternity. With difficulty, Merryl spoke into the stillness. "There are no words . . . I can't say anything." She was wordless, even breathless. The rest of the conversation was like a radiant dream. Merryl said her "goodnight" in a daze and floated into her nightgown and her bed.

A fresh breeze had sprung up, and the softly moving lace curtains kaleidoscoped an endless variety of ethereal patterns on the bedroom wall. Gazing at her ceiling from her pillow, Merryl hovered in the moonlight in a sensation of other worldliness. *I know that's what I'll think of as I lie dying. My last conscious thought in life as I pass over into eternity will be of that poem.*

"Where's the little boy. . ." "Where's the little boy . . ." That was the only phrase left on Merryl's old tape reel of three-year-old Brent saying the Little Boy Blue nursery rhyme. The rest had been mysteriously erased. Tragic as it had seemed at the time, there was something prophetic about it. That little boy had mysteriously disappeared. Where is that little boy? — All grown up and now nurturing his own little boy. Brent had known before she did that he was going to grow up. He had clutched his precious panda bear in that sorrowful realization when he was merely in kindergarten. Brent and Panda Bear had gone through so much together—all the moves and his plastic surgeries after the milk truck accident. Panda was his closest companion till his brother and sisters started coming. Panda Bear lost his ribbon, his little red tongue, an eye, and most of his fleecy fur in the course of their inseparable travels. *How Brent had surprised me with his sage revelation,* Merryl remembered. *Great big tears rolled down his cheeks as I tucked him in that night, as he told me he knew he would be growing up and leaving Panda Bear behind. But I kept Panda in a box under my bed all these years. I'll always keep that little raggedy bear.*

All the moments of life, all the memories, all the pains, all the wishes, all the healings, all the prayers somehow linked together to form life, like a string of beads, beads the color of summer green. Merryl could see it all laid out before her in a graceful curve like beads on a string. She damaged that string when she was so numbed by her own pain that she neglected to receive Brent's boyish sacrifice of love, and she paid a dear price for it all these years. But through the deeply penetrating pain, she tapped into a new depth of love. With this reconciliation and revelation, she felt as if she had found her lost beads.

"Beads means prayers . . ." What had her spirit been telling her? Every prayer is another link of love? Beads of love! That's what lasts.

Merryl turned over toward the lacey shadows on the wall to sleep. She was at peace, an exhausted peace. Somehow, she had done her job and not too badly after all. She had loved, and it hadn't failed. For all her ineptness, it had been enough because it was God, God in her. God is Love.

Sometime in the early dawn of Saturday, Larry crawled in under the sheet beside her, tired from a long night of menial labor and a long drive home. He nudged her awake as he slipped one arm under her shoulder and the other across her waist and drew her tightly to him. Then he snuggled his face into her neck and breathed, "I love you," in a choking whisper. In response, she reached up and closed her hand around the back of his neck. He broke into shaking sobs as she stroked him.

"I need you so much. What would I ever do without you?" he managed to say after a few minutes. "Thank you for putting up with me. I know I've made your life hell at times. Please don't give up on me. I just couldn't make it without you."

Merryl knew he really meant it . . . again. How could she ever give up on him? He is still growing up, too. As Larry fell asleep beneath her arm, her favorite scripture came to her mind—good ole John 16:33: In the world you will have tribulation, but be of good cheer, for I have overcome the world—*for you*. To Merryl that was the summation in a nutshell of all God's truth.

In the dim silence, she recognized the sound of a light rain on the bushes outside the open window. Refreshing rain! She'd have to figure something else to do with her basket of clean, wet towels; they wouldn't dry outside today. But the heat wave was over, like her search for the green glass beads.

Merryl could hear her heart beating in her ear against the pillow. Th-thump, th-thump, th-thump. Her heartbeat sounded strong and steady. For forty-six years it had been beating like that, and it could go on for at least that many more. It sounded like it had a purpose, a reason for beating—to love, just to love. Love is never wasted. Love can never fail.

Merryl's Poetry

Sunshine Days

These summer sunshine days

Always remind me

Of the same golden sun,

Bright blue skies,

Smiling clouds—

Golden times of splashing, laughing

Sparkling fun.

Soft, cool clover between bare toes,

Thickly leafy elms,

Deep green,

And their dark, cool

Sheltered shady circles on the lawn.

Oh, my dolls loved it so—

Their breeze lullabyes—

Those days of richest green,

Brightest gold, and quiet smiles

Of the soul.

Inside Sunshine

I couldn't go outside today
But sadly stayed indoors to play.

While counting raindrops on the glass,
I waited for the hours to pass.

Then Mommy said, "I know what, hon—
Let's count the things you think are fun!"

Like baking some cookies by and by
Or rolling a crust for a chocolate pie!"

"Eating ice cream is what I like best
And wearing my pretty party dress.

Or having some friends to my house for tea—
Just Dolly and Erin and Teddy and me.

Splashing water in the summer sun –
That is always the mostest fun!

'Course, going to Grandma's is nicer than that.
Sometimes she lets me wear her hat.

But the circus was the best time I <u>ever</u> had!
The silly, fat clown made me feel glad.

'Cept not as much as when I sit on your lap
And read a story before my nap.

I love you, Mommy. I'm happy, and – say –
The sun is shining in <u>here</u> today!"

Quantum Leap

I never saw a hockey game;
    I never hoped to see one
Till I came to work for CHL,
    And now I wouldn't miss one.

They asked me if I had a clue
    What the game was all about yet.
I said, "Sure, all they try to do
    Is get the hock into the hock net."

Why they all laughed at what I said
    I couldn't figure out then,
But now I'm at the hockey rink
    Whenever the doors are open.

They sure were right! The game is great!
    I've never seen a better.
I know the players and penalty rules
    Right down to the letter.

Up to this year, ballet was my thing
    For excitement and drama in motion.
But NOW it's the stick and puck on the ice
    That stirs up my blood and emotion!

Merrylynn Cox

My Helper

When the burden's too heavy to push up the hills,
When the money's not enough to cover the bills,
When hard, angry words come too fast,
When dreams of happiness seem long past,
When to lift up to hope my eyes are too weary,
When even the sun turns dark and dreary,
My friend is my work, constant dishes and laundry.
Dust settles my soul from the bleak quandary.
In feeding the children their daily meals,
I find Saving Grace that quietly heals. Amen

The Morning Glory Box

Lost to all time,
Save only to my mind's eye
And my heart's heart.
There I leave it
With one last, longing glance—
The Morning Glory Box,
Sitting on top of the heap,
My treasure, now trash, as I walk away.
Letters of a precious time in my life.
My mother saved them for me to keep.
I am not allowed.
It is moving day.
"Get rid of the debris."
Old Latin books and geometry
Passed down from sister to sister.
Young, funny verses scribed inside the covers,
Memories of teenage days,
Of no value now,
Except to remember.
The wedding presents, never used—
Silver trays, luncheon linen,
Lovely bridal embroidery,
Lily of the Valley,
Too fine for me.

Baby toys outgrown,
Never missed by the babies they had known,
But how they pull at the heartstrings of the mother
To see them sold to another—
The smiling little train I watched follow the pink houseshoes
Around and around the kitchen table—
No one cries after it, no one but me,
"I love you, don't go!
House, Days, Joy,
Don't go from me
Into the past forever!"

The Answer

"I know who You are, Lord—
Guider of stars and planets,
Director of the cells in my veins,
Capable and caring in everything.

I do not doubt You made me, see me, love me,
Have a wish for me to understand that—
To enter the cloud of the glory
You have designed for me.

Gladly I have inhaled the fragrance of Your mercy,
Securely I have nestled silent and small in Your palm,
Bravely I have walked on Your Word of Faith
Across the chasm and found it sturdy.

It is not You I doubt,
Not Your wisdom, not Your power,
Not Your keeping care.
God, . . . it's me — I'm such a lamb.
I don't see well, hear well, think well.
I can't even follow Your Shepherd well.
The stony path is steep; my feet are tiny and weak,
And the shady thicket entices me out of the way.

I'm so small and silly a sheep,
So low on knowing and doing,
On visions and . . . love.
I trust You, but how can You have Your way
In one so foolish as I?
You do all things well,
But I can't see, hear, understand.

My life is in Your hands,
And that's just where I want it to be.
I know You do Your part,
But can I do the little You've left to me?"

In answer, He whispered, "Only in Me."

My Petition

Father, I come to You, Your daughter,
  Knowing Your always enduring kindness,
I bring another who yearns for Your comfort.
  Please kiss my friend.

An innocent man who's been hard pressed,
  He's fighting a foe who hates his life.
He's battered and bloody, so tired and aching.
  Reach out Your hand.

Come breathe divine vapor into his darkness.
  The author of lies has driven him far.
He's lost in a labyrinth with only a sputtering
  Candle to guide him.

Enlighten his heartcave with Your Sonlight.
  From every angle shine Your brilliance.
Drive from his mind the shadows of sorrow
  Show him Yourself.

The weightlessness of Your life let him feel.
  Touch and stroke his thoughts of pain.
With warm tears of love bathe from his wounds
  The blood of battle.

Merrylynn Cox

Draw him into Your chamber of praises,
　　Limitless, sparkling with crystalline music,
Iridescent air and soft pearl shimmer.
　　Refresh his soul.

Garment him in Your gold and purple.
　　Robe him in Your boundless grace.
Crown him with Your laurel garland,
　　Victor of Faith.

Ascension

I love sitting with you, but I love growing more.
If I grow while you sit, we grow apart.
Can you feel me tugging at the string?
I apologize for being filled with lightness;
I didn't design my being.

You reach as I rise like a balloon ascending,
But your energy is expended to pull me down.
Arresting, you would hold back my flight,
Keep the bright souvenir for yourself.

But come, let us fly together.
Reach with me into the daring air.
Place your foot with mine upon the vapor stair.
Trust your weight to solid reality—the ageless Dreamrock
    there.

You say you love me and need me, yet can this be?
You intend to tether my destiny.
I am the more deceived.
Shall I also go mad for love
And float mindless on the stream of drowned dreams,
The petals of my gathered beauties languishing limp and
    withering?
Shall I mourn all my days for the lost heavenlies?

I am Shakespeare's sister!
Don't laugh; I have prayed to be.
I won't die so young.
I have things to say; work to be done.

You would consume all my substance to be nourished by it.
I am not a wafer for you to eat.
I cannot break myself any longer for you.
But there is One Who has given
Living Bread to strengthen us both.
He ascended, and so must we.
Real love desires me to be all I can be.

Why do you sit and let the adventure pass?
I bob in the eddy of breezes
Restless to soar, to dance in the clouds.
If you've never gone dancing,
Can I hope you understand? Alas!

If you can love me for what I am,
We will both be the better for it.
If you cannot, only remember . . .
Once I was content there, but I cannot stay where I was.
Courage unstifled, I have lifted my eyes.
Buoyant, my feet no longer touch the ground.

You say I'll regret leaving you behind.
I know it's true. Yes, I very much mind.
I am misunderstood.
It is only that I long to see life from the air;
My thought is not to sever.

Sitting is good for a while
But not forever.
I must go . . .
    The gravity of the sky
        Summons irresistibly.
           It possibly could be
               You sat too long for me.

Merrylynn Cox

Descent
(Response to Ascension)

The hell you say,
You pompous bitch!
You have to go?
Then scratch that itch.

You think I care?
You'll never know.
Go walk on air—
Winds blow, I'll blow.

You're free to fly,
But the win is mine.
Go live your lie;
I'll be just fine!

So the touch I bring
Just holds you down?
I've got no string,
This cuts it, clown!

Do I sound mad?
Don't kid yourself.
You've made me glad
I'm off your shelf.

Shakespeare indeed!
You're just a nut.
You want a degree?
Well, kiss my butt.

That piece of paper
Won't keep you warm.
You'll see up there,
I did no harm.

I may be a jewel
In the rough,
But you're flat cruel;
Clear enough?

This sitting shit
Is over today.
Good! Go do it!
I head away.

Find your heaven—
I wish you well.
Think of me
As I reign in hell.

Merrylynn Cox

Don't Smile

Pain is bearable,
Nothing to fear.
It's borne all around us.
See all the tears.

Young and old,
Foul and Fair,
Innocent and guilty,
Have all been there.

Over all the world,
So much, so constant,
But today is different:
It's me, the recipient.

How can you smile;
Can't you see?
The bearer now
Of the pain is ME.

Flying to Albuquerque

Is it really over God,
Receding into the distance
As the mountains of Santa Fe?
I left my heart and my hopes there.

Adobe looks unnatural in snow.
Only the pines fit in.
Will either of us ever fit in again?

We were misfits in the world.
When we found each other,
We were sure the solace for life
Resided in this other;
Loneliness was over.
We were so young.

The devil was so jealous!
What God put together,
He would do everything
To put asunder.

I don't want to go on alone.
Our hearts and spirits are intertwined
So inextricably after so many years.
I'll never be whole
With so much of my life missing.

Merrylynn Cox

But this is the lesson of the pain:
The worst is being together,
Being the sounding board for his anger and distress.
I could not soothe the fear that knows no bounds.
My peace was ineffective against hell's anxiety.
My forgiveness could not expiate his guilt.
God, you are the only One left Who can.
I'm gone, without his kiss or smile.

I want to put my arms around him
And just hold him, letting him know, again,
It can be all right.
But it's so complicated,
And I just can't bear his rebuff . . . again.

What's the use?
There's too much hurt there to wade through.
Our hearts are drowning;
They tread water, looking for a savior
Till they're exhausted.
We can't go on like this.

But look, the snow is only on the
North side of the mountains.
The other is clear.
There is hope. Tears wait.

His Tears

My veins weep. My pores seep tears.
Ah, agony for people, people, people,
    People—
Solitary, seeking, sinking,
Lonely, losing, lost,
Lost and more lost,
    Loster! Lostest!!!
Where, when, what, and
Most of all why, Why and WHY?
What is the answer for people?
Is there a question?
Is there a reason for the blood?
    the pain, the fatigue,
    the anguish . . . the Lostness?

Oh man, discouraged, sad, mad,
So penniless, so alone.
A number, a code, no place, no value.
Why do they hound you for your life?
    money, strength, love?
It's spent. All spent.
No reserve, none.
No warm substance to fill the inner emptiness.
No warm rest with pillows and arms
    to cushion and enfold the hurting.

Merrylynn Cox

Ah, woman, adrift, exhausted,
    on your own,
Digging at the mountain with a fragile plastic spoon.
Sweeping waves off a rock with a shabby nylon broom.
What can you do? No one cares.
The dark sea is billowing,
    made high and noisy by harsh winds and words.
Your beauty is stolen.
If you die, you die.
But who will feed the children?

I ache for you, child—
What do you know, so small?
Eyes so trusting, looking to one who's weaker yet,
Full of fear, clinging to one more frightened.
You can live if you can find a shred of love,
    a crust of comfort.
There is none; it's bare, all gone.
The larger leans on the smaller for support, crushing.
    And you can never understand,
    Only forgive, and hate;
    Love and despair.
Why were you born?
Why do you have needs that demand and drain?
It's your fault, they say.
They take out their pain on you.
The destroyer tromps through your tiny bones and tender
    flesh.

Oh world, will you hunger till you eat filth?
Will you continue to scavenge for scraps in the dark, empty
places?
I was One of you.
I lived, loved among you, gave all for you.
My Life Is For Everyone.
Be refreshed at the crimson stream.
My veins weep for you. My pores seep tears.

I Prayed in L.A. One Day

At the foot of the Hollywood Hills
In the warm California sun
I designed my fantasy prayer room.

The palms, pines, and cypresses
Watched approvingly,
Waiting to clap their hands until
The day we are all preparing for.

They were so friendly and supportive,
Smiling quietly and joyfully on my thoughts.

They blessed me on my way,
Saying they would never forget me and that day.
They asked me to remember that contented spot always
And take it with me from there everywhere.

Enforced Musings

Women learn to change things.
Diapers
Attitudes
Oil
Values
Anything that needs changing.

So few the poets
So few the men
And fewer the women
Who see beyond the busy,
The hours and hours
And days and days,
And see the ways of the molecules,
The wisps of invisible time,
As they curl about our lovely limbs
And carry us off.

Merrylynn Cox

The Gift of Gold

Wings on the crisp wind,
Golden leaves fly and flutter down.
I delight in them as they rejoice before me.
Like a shower of coins from out of Heaven,
They come to rest like
A burst of sudden wealth at my feet.
With little thought in my bliss
Of where destiny is calling them,
The golden leaves flutter in flamboyant death,
All to eternal glory, that is certain.
I sense a promise of bounty,
Riches of abounding grace.

St. Valentine's Day of Love

I saw the somber man in the wheel chair,
Sitting in the chilly wind at the bus stop,
Give to the prideless man who had been rummaging in the
    trash can
Two cigarettes.
The shabby man said, "Thank you," and went on.

Who saw? Me and God.

On this day of hearts and flowers,
Sappy sentiments,
Shiny red satin boxes full of sweets for sweethearts.
Words of "I love you" on pretty cards,
    Tender
    Comic
    Sincere
    Or ingratiating,
Serving someone else,
Mostly ourselves,
Doing our duty

– to whom?
The Commandment: Love one another?
Our "neighbor?"

I thought, "How sad,
To have no pride left at all,"
But I didn't give him a dime.

A Sun Departed

Eyes, a hazy sky of gray,
Hair, prairie wheat on a summer day.
Smile so rare, a burst of grace,
Sunshine brilliance in his face.
    Soul grasping universe longingly,
    Spirit reaching starward soaringly.

A quick wit to stump and stun,
Humor to delight the sun.
Anger flashing as lightning above,
Heart smoldering eternal love.
    Walking before me glowingly,
    With Jesus he winked knowingly.

A laugh to set wood a-prancing,
Dreams all dressed up for dancing.
Gifted with a promised greatness,
Burdened by a deep aloneness.
    Drew from the Vine succulently.
    Grew to dwell here reluctantly.

Named Lebanon Cedar at his birth,
Called to Creator from dull earth,
Treasured by God as true friend,
His life was much too soon to end.
    Day turned to dark thunderously,
    But promised to come again gloriously!

On Reading Anne Bradstreet,

America's First Woman Poet

What a remarkable and blessed woman
To have the muse awakened within her
That might have lain dormant forever
But for the careful placement of her birth.

I claim that fortunate circumstance of placement for my
own life.
I have been slowly maturing in a secret crevice
Until the life-giving star reaches its precise apex
And sends its golden laser ray to awaken the fully-seasoned bud.

I tremble with potential energy for the signal to burst into
bloom!
Here comes that ray over the crest of the cliff into my
shadowy nursery.
I am ready to bless the few or many who chance on the rare glory
Forming inside my eager, fragrant, trembling petals.

Only a few more moments now till it bursts forth!

Merrylynn Cox

Heart's Home

Sunlight on salad in the time-honored kitchen beside the
    lasagna leavings,
A trilling musical giggle of the fourth generation, delighting
    from the old girlhood bedroom,
The air lovingly grasped by the long-standing walls breathes
    memories, old and new, all cherished.
This cloud — this aura — is where my heart belongs —
    Why I've never strayed very far from the core,
Blessed to be allowed back to cuddle again between the
    covers of my perhaps imagined cozy youth,
Safe from the confusing, astonishing present where I seem
    to always be a stranger.

Tulsa for Me

Old Tulsey Town was her first Indian name,
Growing up on Arkansas River's plain.
Tales of teepees, cowboys, oil gusher days,
Gained her our love and earned her our praise.

From years of work in the tallest tower in town,
I've met many people from the world around—
Engineers from London, field techs from Saudi,
Correspondents from the isles of Hawaii.

When they've lived in Paris, Caracas, or Rome,
Where do they seek to make their home
When all their working days are through,
And their time of rest and reward is due?

Having stayed in my city in their world travels,
So many are drawn back as time unravels—
Back to that center-of-America spot—
The city marked TULSA by the map's dot.

No other place offers them so much—
Big city culture with a small-town touch—
Schools, industry, parks, sports, and art,
Prime theater and ballet set Tulsa apart.

Merrylynn Cox

Affordable homes, stores, and honest banks.
For alphabetical streets, the planners get thanks!
All the conveniences you ever want to find
And the warmth of a neighborhood heart and mind.

She has the right climate—not too much heat or cold
And attractive buildings, both new and old.
She's not too big, and she's not too small.
There's a nook and lifestyle for each and all.

Those who've traveled the world appreciate her best—
So clean and beautiful. (They've seen the rest!)
They know beyond those who've never roamed
The special features of their chosen home.

I've traveled a bit, too, but I returned for a part
Of the one bright city that has won my heart.
She has everything for me, I've come to see,
And old Tulsey Town suits me to a "T"!

Becoming a Big Sister

When I was a baby and brand new
There was really a big To Do!
My mommy and daddy were so proud.
"The best present ever!" Mommy said out loud.
She dressed me in Great Granny's dress and bonnet.
At church I got a book with my name on it.
We laughed! I was happy and grew and grew,
But one day before I was even two,
Mommy said, "Guess what is in my tummy"
And started to tell me someone was coming.
I wonder how it feels to have a baby inside.
I stuck dolly under my shirt for a ride!
It took a lot longer than you might think,
But one day my Mimi came to fix my drink.
She said Mommy had a big surprise,
And I might not even believe my eyes.
Mommy had gone to get our new baby.
"We'll go meet her, O,K?" " . . . maybe."
Mommy and Daddy seemed really glad
And kinda busy, but I wasn't too mad.

Merrylynn Cox

She was little and squirmy, a lot like my dolly,
But they brought her to my house! What for? Oh, golly!
Mimi, Auntie and Unkie, they goo and fuss so,
But hey! I'm your baby. She has to go!
"Where Eyan come from? Where did we get her?"
"She grew in my tummy. I showed you, remember?"
Is she cuter than me? She makes so much noise!
And everyone brings her presents and toys.
Mommy's so busy, and I want to play.
I'm sad and feel left out all day.
Mommy says when she's bigger, I'll like her a lot.
She is pretty cute, but she took my spot!
I'd like to be friends. I'll give her a chance,
And when she grows some, I'll teach her to dance!
Now we're such good sisters and dance a lot
At our ballet place. It's Mimi's favorite spot.
A good fairy or angel I can't always be,
But I thank God for my wonderful family!

Our Aunt Bessie

My mother's sister is as dear to me
As even my own sister can be.
Each time she visits is a special delight.
We hug her and kiss her with all our might.

She always brings something fun to do
And teaches us a new thing or two.
But just being with her is the mostest fun.
She always lets us romp and run!

We climb and flip and make a ruckus,
Then she dresses us up like a duchess!
Her imagination is fun and wild
To thrill and entertain any child.

Seven Heaven is her high-up home
And one of our favorite places to roam.
She has treats and movies and high-heeled shoes
And great big windows with high-up views.

We love her "Dorothy" and her bowl of rocks
And all the silly hats in her box.
Taking our pictures is her favorite thing
in special clothes with a little *Bling*.

Merrylynn Cox

We can be angels or elves or princesses fair.
With her camera she has a special flare.
Maybe next year we'll even sit still,
And then she'll remember us in her will!

Of her our memories will be the best,
Of balloons and laughter, a daily fun fest.
She fills our lives with glitter and gleam.
Of a better aunt one could never dream.

My Boy
by Maxx

Ever since I was a sprat
OK Street is where it's at.
Scotty is my chosen boy
And every day my chief-est joy!

When I was too little to climb the step
He was my ever-constant help.
Through fireworks and encroaching threat
He was my buddy and safety net.

Now that I'm as big as my bark
I protect HIM in daylight and dark.
He says I'm lots better than any gal
And there never could be a better pal!

I share his dinner, his bed, and TV.
Every day he depends on me.
When he's good I take him for walks,
And we have nice, long silent talks.

Merrylynn Cox

I give him back what I can –
Fistfuls of hair in his hand.
When he's sad, I make him feel better.
I know Good Dog Rules to the letter.

Rides in his truck and trips to the park
Make our times a happy lark.
I'm smart and wise, a special dog.
He knows that I'm his gift from God!

My Daughter, My Friend

God's Princess of Renown, Her Forty Years Have Earned Her an Eternal Crown

My baby daughter brightens my life; she is such a lovely mother and wife,

But her value to me is more to the end that she is a fun and fabulous friend.

Born at home, as a planned "surprise," she proved to be the greatest prize.

I never expected to have number four, but she just made me want some more.

We called her "our little shepherdess," as she tried to care for all the rest.

She took the hand of her big brother and led him like a little mother,

Matching up his shoes and socks; she's stable as a mountain of rocks.

"Positively correlated" was her name, and she has well lived up to the same.

Starting school, she was always so tall, her sports records still stand on the gym wall.

In her picture, she looks like the teacher. For achievements, no one could reach her.

What she overcame is quite a list. Many words can only tell the gist:

Big brother's teases, Daddy's rages. I could go on and on for pages.

Took out the trash, washed tons of dishes while making her own list of wishes.

Threw papers, babysat, waited on tables. Didn't ever wear designer labels!

Saved all her money to buy her first car and then hitched it to a far away star.

It took her to college, a mighty long haul, and for a Master's degree she answered the call.

Then a real job was a big hurdle—trials and troubles to make the blood curdle.

But a tougher kid I've never seen. In her eye is a determined gleam.

Yet she always has a hearty laugh no matter how the hard times chaff.

Honest and straightforward through and through, be sure she'll do as she wants you to.

Everyone she meets is her eternal friend. To some she's an angel to the end.

She has a strong faith, and she needs it, too—nothing she does is easy to do!

At last she found her everlasting Hon. Third try hubby was the one!

She had to wait so many years to finally birth her darling dears.

Those beautiful babes—a dream come true. But Heaven should send an extra arm or two!

Two very different lovely little girls make her life merry dual whirls.

Between job, school, Tulsa Run, Spirit Week, stress and fatigue always threaten to peak.

With swimming, gymnastics, twice-weekly ballet, to catch a breath there is just no way!

Yet the daily routine of rush and run still gives the family lots of laughs and fun.

In the screaming, when there's a pause, they find for love there's always cause.

Her girls get mommy cuddles galore, and sweet dolls and toys cover their floor.

Daddy takes them on trips to lots of fun places and puts happy smiles on their pretty faces.

A hardworking mom, a day never fails when she has to be as hard as nails.

But just like fluffy marshmallow goo, she is so soft and mushy, too.

In Grandmother's home, she knows she's blessed. In securing God's best, she's passed every test.

Her husband and girls give her constant praise. She is treasured by all for all of her days.

The Silly Kitty Saga

Two Christmas kittens are such a delight!
Sweet, hungry Clover, but Chloe can bite!
In happy bliss for four and a half years,
The new arrival brought them to tears!
Mr. Daisy (was supposed to be a girl),
His busy antics made their fur curl!
He bounces and dashes and eats like crazy!
But how the girls LOVE their Mr. Daisy!
Then came Pepper, a tuxedo cat sweetie!
Erin picked the cutest new sister kitty.
Poor Rescue Mazie had to go back;
She picked a mean fight with every cat!
But Tucker Girl (supposed to be a boy)
Brought to the household brand new joy!
All Miranda's T-shirts prove she's smitten.
She's on her way to her millionth kitten!

Printed in the United States
By Bookmasters